God Notes

Daily Doses of
Divine Encouragement

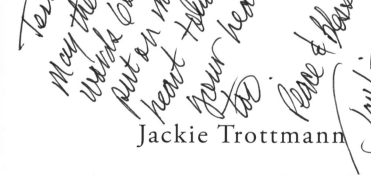

Terri,

May the words God put on my heart touch your heart too.

Peace & Blessings,

Jackie Trottmann

Jackie Trottmann

God Notes: Daily Doses of Divine Encouragement
© 2017 Jackie Trottmann. All rights reserved.

Published in the USA by:
DreamSculpt Books – an imprint of Waterside Productions
www.DreamSculpt.com

Printed in the United States of America
ISBN   978-1-945949-29-6 paperback
                978-1-945949-30-2 ebook

Book & cover design by Darlene Swanson • www.van-garde.com

Contents

Introduction

God is the God of surprises, showing up when we least expect it. *God Notes* was a complete surprise too. That's why I wanted to share the story behind *God Notes*. It's not the story of a book, but rather the story of experiencing God's presence in a very real and personal way.

I first experienced God's presence, of all places, on my morning commute. This holy encounter happened eleven months after leaving my past-life behind.

I was a successful advertising executive in a twenty-year marriage with a young son. Along with the career came the benchmarks of that success: dream home, luxury cars, jewelry, designer clothes, and an active social calendar. Life was extremely stressful, but I dismissed the stress because I had achieved all of my (outward) lofty goals. This life came crashing down one day when my choir director said five words to me.

Before I share those five words, you should know how I was introduced to God. That introduction was made through my mother. She took me to church when I was a little girl. My mother had a strong faith. When the subject of religion came up and the question was asked, what religion are you, my mother would always reply, "I am a broad-minded Baptist." My mother reached out to everyone. She was very broad-minded thanks to her exposure to various religions being raised by a Jewish father and Catholic mother.

Growing up, church was a safe haven for me. My father was an alcoholic. He was later diagnosed with bipolar disorder. His angry outbursts were frightening. He verbally and sometimes physically abused my mother. When I wasn't in school, I practically lived at church. We had a very active youth group that provided shelter away from the unstable atmosphere at home. It helped me to survive and thrive.

After high school, many of my friends left to go to college or moved away. I found the repeated messages from the pulpit oppressive: heaven was the prize, and in this life we would suffer. There was little talk of joy.

My image of God was the great, judgmental scorekeeper in the sky that I feared would squish me like a bug if I stepped out of line. Like many fledgling adults, I left home to venture out on my own. I also left the church and my faith behind.

When my son was seven years old, I had a strong desire to find a church home. I found it in First Presbyterian Church in Kirkwood, Missouri. It's been home ever since.

The year was now 2001. I was in my choir director's office. It was during a one-on-one voice lesson when my choir director abruptly stopped, turned to me, looked me in the eye and barked, "Why won't you let go!" Those were the five words.

He was talking about my *voice*, not my *life*. But that's all it took for me to face the truth. I knew why I wasn't letting go. My soul was dying. The true essence of Jackie was a hollow shell. I was successful on the outside and spiritually bankrupt on the inside.

I knew something had to change. After much soul-searching, I left my marriage, dream home, and career. I moved to a small rental house in October 2002. I was unemployed and down to my last nickel in the checking account.

During this time of soul-searching my pastor gave a sermon on prayer. He said that prayer was talking to God, just like these words are talking to you on this page. I had never thought of prayer in that way. So, I began to *talk to God* more often.

January 2003 marked the start of a new life. I was given a dream job as Vice President of Marketing for a company that helped faith-based and not-for-profit organizations raise funds.

The job had a forty-five-minute commute each way. In the mornings, I would talk to God. During that time, I had trouble sleeping. I would wake up in the middle of the night and pray for people until I fell back to sleep.

It was August 30, 2003. I will always remember that date because my life truly changed forever. That's the day I experienced God's presence for the first time.

I was talking to God on my morning commute. In a silly voice I said, "I think You are waking me up in the middle of the night because You want me to talk to You."

Right after I said those words I felt like the wind had been knocked out of me, only this was an amazingly pleasant feeling. I was rendered speechless and was filled with an unbelievable sense of divine love. It was euphoric. I didn't want it to end. The feeling lasted for twenty minutes.

As I took the exit ramp, all I could think of was what the apostle Paul says, "All things become new." I felt like a new creation.

In November 2003, I had my first intimate experience of God speaking to me.

I had romantically reconnected with a friend from kindergarten at a high school reunion in August. He was the first Christian man I had dated since my college days. He introduced me to a book called *Wild at Heart* by John Eldridge. The book so spoke to me because it addresses the father wounds that exist for so many. The book described the desires that men and women have and how God gave us those desires.

My friend encouraged me to attend a live Ransomed Heart retreat for women in Colorado. The enrollment was by a lottery method. I entered my application and was chosen.

It was at the conference where God spoke to me. At one of the sessions it was said, "Either the men in our lives bring us to God or drive us to God." My friend had certainly driven me to God! I say that because a wide gulf was beginning to form between us. We both had unhealed wounds from prior marriages and relationships. While the greatest commandment is to, *love the Lord your God with all your heart, and with all your soul, and with all your mind,* I wasn't doing that. I realized that I was seeking love so desperately that I wasn't allowing God to love me either. If I was being truthful, this desperation was also pushing my friend away.

After one of the sessions we were asked to find a quiet place to contemplate what we had heard. I chose to go outside. It was snowing. The retreat complex was nestled in the mountains. The mountains were blanketed in white and shimmered with the newly fallen snow. The views were magnificent, stunning. Only God could have created a scene so majestic. I sat under an awning and absorbed the view. All was still. The only sound was the wind blowing through the evergreen trees.

In this stillness God said to me, "I delight in you, I will fight for you, you are beautiful. I will never change. I will be the same today and tomorrow." It seemed that in every significant male relationship I had in my life, that person had changed. God made it clear that His love for me would not change.

For once, I wasn't looking at the mountains and the magnitude of it all and wishing to be with a man. I was there with God. It was so lovely, and I rested in God's arms and admired God's creation and the wonder and splendor. I felt safe. I felt whole. I felt at peace. I felt loved.

I returned from the retreat with a reclaimed heart. I intentionally did not use the word changed because I believe we change from the original state in which God created us, out of pure love. We allow the world to make us forget Whose we are.

That November, God brought Robert Trottmann into my life. We married nine months later. Our relationship is a true spiritual partnership where we love God, love our neighbor (try to do our best), and love ourselves.

My dream job collapsed. The company went out of business. I went back into the hectic radio advertising business from which I had left. I continued to talk to God, but I wasn't doing much listening! After one crazy work day too many, I turned to meditation to keep from losing my mind. In the past I thought that meditation *was doing nothing*. I didn't have time to do nothing. But after trying it one day, I was hooked. The anxiety and stress I was feeling immediately went away. I understood what the psalmist said when he wrote: *Be still and know that I am God,* Psalm 46:10.

I have learned that God's language is silence and God speaks to us in stillness. My life was so transformed through meditation that I created meditation CDs to help others learn to be still and quiet the mind.

Fast-forward to January 2014. Through prayer and stillness, I experienced God speaking. This time, it was not on a mountain top but in the office of my home.

I had signed up for a month-long prayer retreat offered through our church. At the first meeting we were given the following instructions: each day when we woke up, we were to say, "I'm on retreat." I loved that! We were encouraged to say this throughout the day and before we went to sleep. We were told to have fun, let God love you, welcome God to show up, and pay attention.

It was six years since I left the corporate workplace. Without a morning commute, I spent and continue to spend the first two to three hours each day reading, writing, journaling, praying, or meditating. These are my spiritual practices.

The second day into the prayer retreat I asked God to give me a word for the day. For several years I had the desire to publish a daily devotional with a word for the day. When I first entered the advertising business, I asked the media director for a new word each day. I learned the advertising business one word at a time.

While I champion the importance of meditation, I knew that others may not choose to invest ten to twenty minutes a day to be still to be in God's presence; but, surely, I thought, they would have time for a word!

I started prayer that day with telling God my heart's desires. It was once again the start of a New Year. I was filled with new hope and promise. I then settled down to stillness, letting go of all thoughts except for one final request. I asked, God, "What is my word today?" God answered. God said, "Believe."

The word believe started to tumble out in what had to be fifty sentences. I wanted to stop and write them down, but they were coming so fast. I didn't want to break the flow. The feeling was very similar to the experience in the car. What I did manage to capture was this:

Believe you are loved,
Believe you are worthy,
Believe you are able,
Believe it's your time,
Believe I am yours,
Believe you are mine,
I believe in you.

While God continued to give more words to me, I felt led to pull 365 words out of the Bible. I would sit in the mornings and look over the words until I felt inspired – the word inspire literally means in Spirit. My eyes would randomly land on a word and I would start writing the words that God spoke to me.

Many times, other words would come to mind that weren't on the list. This process continued for almost two years.

The timeline was not mine. A funny story to prove this fact was the day I decided to write at the Missouri Botanical Garden. I told Robert I thought it would be a beautiful place to go and write. That day it rained. It wasn't a soft rain. It was a torrential downpour that lasted all day.

I suggested to Robert that we have lunch at a restaurant where he had never been. In the midst of our meal, I came up with another plan. We would go to the remodeled downtown St. Louis Public Library. Robert had never seen it and it is a beautiful place. What better, quieter place to write than a library, no?

We drove to the library in the pouring rain. After giving Robert a quick tour, I picked the perfect room to settle in. I took out all of my materials to write. Instead of the atmosphere being quiet like you'd expect a library to be, in walked a boisterous librarian who talked non-stop with a co-worker. Undeterred, I moved to a different room. The same scenario happened. It happened four times in four different rooms! I laughed and said to God, "I got the message!" *Inspiration is not turned on like a faucet. God speaks to us in silence or stillness, not usually on demand.*

Interesting to note is that the most words I ever wrote in a day was when I was really sick. I could hardly get out of bed because I felt so depleted. However, in this weakened state, God gave me loving words of encouragement and inspiration.

There is definitely a theme going on here as I write this introduction. It is another New Year. The reading at church was on the baptism of Jesus. Luke 3:21-22: *Now when all the people were baptized, and when Jesus also had been baptized and was praying, the heaven was opened, and the Holy Spirit descended upon him in bodily form like a dove. And a voice came from heaven, "You are my Son, the Beloved; with you I am well pleased."* NRSV

Robert and I were in a spiritual direction class that morning. We meditated over the text and shared our thoughts. Robert said, "Jesus hadn't done anything in his ministry and yet, God is pleased."

I took out my notes from the Ransomed Heart retreat from thirteen years ago and read: *If Jesus had to hear approval from His Father, how much more do we need to hear approval as well?*

We all need love, approval, and recognition. It's obvious that the first place we should receive it is from our own mothers and fathers. Our mothers and fathers have a huge impact on our lives.

In my case, I know now that my father was not in his right mind. My mother did her best to cope and stay strong. However, it is still very painful to know I will never hear the words, "I'm proud of you," from my parents.

But I *do* hear those words from *God*, the Creator of the entire universe, the Creator of *me*. I *am* the beloved. God *is* pleased with me.

I trust that these *God Notes* will give *you* the same peace, joy, and encouragement that they have given to me. May you know these words, "*You are my beloved*, with *you* I am well pleased." Because that is who you are – a unique and precious child of God.

~ *Jackie Trottmann*

Using God Notes

The notes have been put into chapter themes. When we pay attention, God speaks to us through nature (Chapter 1 – Nature), our body (Chapter 2 – Body), our mind (Chapter 3 – Mind), our spirit (Chapter 4 – Spirit).

God leads and guides us through many ways (Chapter 5 – Guidance), and restores us through healing (Chapter 6 – Healing).

God empowers us through transformation (Chapter 7 – Transformation) and eases our burdens and frees us through truth (Chapter 8 – Truth).

What was surprising to me was that in assembling the manuscript, I found that many of the words took on a form that might start by mentioning nature, then the mind, body, spirit, and lead into healing, transformation, and end with truth.

So, these chapter groupings have not lost the spontaneity of the daily words. You can start at the beginning or pick a chapter that speaks to you. The only reading requirement is to be open and to listen.

Dedication

Everyone needs someone to believe in them. Thank you, Robert, for believing in me. Thank you for your love, sharing our faith together, and for your constant support. You've made my dreams come true. *You* are a dream come true.

Chapter 1

Nature

I am the Great Artist, and all of creation is My greatest masterpiece. I didn't keep it for Myself, I gave it to you.

There was darkness until My Spirit moved over the face of the waters. Then I said, "Let there be light"; and there was light. I stepped back to appraise My work that first day. And it was good.

Then I created the sky and the dry land. Things were coming together. I looked at My work that second day. And it was good.

Then I said, "Let there be plants of every kind bearing fruit." And, again, it was good.

Then I said, "Let there be lights in the sky to separate the day from the night. Let them be for signs and for seasons and for days and years. Let them shed light on the earth."

There needed to be more, so I made two great lights, the greater light to rule by day and the lesser light to rule by night along with stars. Yes, it was moving along nicely. And it was good.

Then I created all the creatures of the sea and the birds of the air. And it was good. I even blessed them and said, "Be fruitful and multiply."

Then I created all the living creatures great and small, of every kind on the earth. And it was good.

Then I saved the best for last. I said, "Let's make humankind in Our image. And I will give them dominion over everything that moves on the earth."

So, I created man and woman in My own image. And I gave everything to them and their future generations. I blessed them and said, "Be fruitful and multiply. I give everything to you." And it wasn't just good, it was very good.

It is still very good. *You* are good.

Abundance

My abundance is all around you.

There is an abundance of air to breathe, an abundance of sights and sounds from nature to listen to and behold.

There is an abundance of opportunities waiting for you when you stop, listen, and pay attention.

When you seek to receive My abundance,

I will shower upon you an abundance of love, joy, strength, and peace.

I am your God, the God of abundance.

For you, nothing is in short supply.

Awe

Never lose your sense of awe and wonder.

If busyness and overwhelm consume your life, you miss the awe of the world's grandeur and miracles.

There is the awe of new life from a baby to a butterfly.

There is the awe of the sunrise and sunset. Never are there two of the same!

Be in awe of your body. It functions without you having to think.

Your heart beats, your lungs breathe, your metabolism works 24 hours a day.

I am in awe of all My creation.

That means I am in awe of you.

Beauty

When your soul feels empty, feed it beauty.

Drink in the beauty of the sky, a flower, a sunset, a tree.

In the material world beauty is seen on the outside.

This beauty is short-lived and fickle.

In My world beauty is everlasting and seen within:

Beauty in kindness,

Beauty in compassion,

Beauty in humility.

See beyond the outside beauty and see the beauty within others.

Allow My beauty to shine forth through you.

Birds

L ook at the birds.

They come in many sizes and many colors just like My children.

Birds don't spend their days building elaborate houses.

Birds find shelter and protection in My trees.

Birds do not gather food or possessions, because I provide for their needs.

Birds sing bird songs of joy all day long.

Birds fly free over tree tops and roof tops towards the clouds.

I provide for the birds.

I provide for you.

When you trust Me, your heart and spirit will feel light as a bird's feather.

Blessing

Life is a blessing.

I hold no blessing back from anyone.

Each day My blessing of the sun shining upon the earth is offered.

I give My blessing of the trees and the flowers and all of creation to you.

Receive My blessing to live in peace.

Receive My blessing to live in abundance.

Receive My blessing to risk and to live your life to the fullest.

Because you have received My blessing, be a constant blessing to others.

Cloud

The rain cloud is necessary to refresh and foster growth.

The storm cloud never stays for long.

It is a reminder to seek shelter in Me.

Don't let thoughts of anxiety or confusion cloud your judgment.

Turn over those thoughts to Me and I will make things clear.

Don't have your head in the clouds.

It is good to dream dreams.

But you must also take action.

On the other hand, worry, doubt, and fear will cast a dark cloud over you.

Change your thoughts to, "I'm grateful for …" That dark cloud will disappear.

Darkness

Darkness serves several purposes. One purpose is rest. In the darkness, your body lies down to renew with the rest of all creation.

Darkness serves another purpose in not being able to see the path in front of you.

I am working in your favor and don't wish for you to see what's up ahead.

I want you to live in the present moment.

I want you to wait and trust in Me.

Hold My hand and I will lead you through the darkness.

Coming out of the darkness you can appreciate the glorious light.

Darkness is necessary.

Darkness never lasts forever.

My light will always banish the darkness.

Eagle

The eagle is a symbol of power and strength.

The eagle is known for its flight and clear vision.

Eagles are majestic in their appearance.

You are greater than an eagle.

Each day I will renew your strength like an eagle.

Your spirit, when you let go of doubt, fear, and worries, will soar like an eagle.

I provide every need for the eagle.

I will provide for you and more.

Enjoy

I created the world for you to enjoy.

Enjoy its beauty and splendor.

I created *you* with gifts and talents so that when you fully use them, you will enjoy your work and enjoy prosperity.

I enjoy watching you grow.

I want you to enjoy a long, happy, healthy, life.

When you come to Me with your burdens,

you will enjoy peace and live your life with ease.

Everywhere

Everywhere you look, My handiwork is visible.

Everywhere you turn, My creation surrounds you.

When you seek help, people and resources will come from everywhere to assist you.

My eyes are everywhere and see everything.

Know that everywhere you go, I go with you.

Flow

Your life will take on an effortless flow when you trust in Me as your Source.

As a river flows continuously and smoothly, your life will have this same flow.

When you immerse yourself in My loving presence, My Spirit will emerge through you.

You may hit some snags along the way, but it is impossible to be stuck for very long when you stay in the current of My love.

Let go and go with the flow, the flow of oneness with Me.

Glory

For now, the only way to see My glory is through My handiwork.

Heaven and earth are full of My glory.

The stars shine in glory.

The mountains and oceans extend My glory across the earth.

My glory is expressed on every human face.

I have destined you for glory.

My power and glory shine from within you.

Grateful

My creation responds in grateful praise.

Birds sing a grateful song each morning.

Flowers open their petals stretching out in grateful bliss receiving the warmth of the sun.

A grateful heart is a happy heart.

A grateful heart is a heart at peace.

When you focus your mind on what you are grateful for, you become one with Me and all of grateful creation.

Growth

Growth happens over time.

You cannot rush a baby's growth.

You cannot rush the oak tree to reach its full height quickly.

Spiritual growth means nurturing your soul.

Your soul is where your true essence and power resides.

Growth happens in fertile soil.

Growth happens when deep roots form as an anchor.

Without deep roots, the storms will knock you over and uproot you.

Growth happens when a plant is pruned.

Through the process of pruning, old-growth is cut away to make way for the new.

Your growth will continue when you stay rooted in Me.

Lovely

Look around you today and focus on what is lovely.
A lovely flower,
A lovely word said or read,
A lovely breeze against your skin,
A lovely gesture from someone,
A lovely cloud.

When you focus on the lovely you begin to see through My eyes.

Mighty

The mighty redwoods,

The mighty seas,

The mighty mountains,

All illustrate My strength and majesty.

Mighty winds, rains, and waves illustrate My power.

Because My power is within you, you can do mighty things.

Be mighty careful how you use it.

I am your mighty Rock and Protector.

Lean on Me for strength and power.

Miracles

You may only think of a miracle as an event like My Son turning water into wine or Moses parting the Red Sea.

But miracles happen all the time. How does a seed produce a massive oak tree?

How do infinitesimal chromosomes turn into a baby?

How does the tulip die at the end of spring only to return the next spring as bright and beautiful year after year?

All miracles.

The human body is a miracle, healing itself, keeping you alive without you having to think about it.

You are a miracle.

You are unique, marvelous, and wonderful.

When you trust in Me, I can help you live a miraculous life.

People you need to help you will show up. Events become divinely organized.

Believe in miracles, all kinds of miracles, big and small.

Mother

You may use the word Father when you think of Me.

But I want you to think of Me as Mother too.

A mother only knows what it is like to carry a child in her womb.

There is a special bond of love that can never be broken.

Like a mother caring for her developing child, I care for you. I was with you in your mother's womb.

Like a mother hen gathering her chicks under her wings for shelter, I shelter you from life's storms.

Like a fierce mother grizzly bear, I protect you from others who wish to harm you.

Like a caring mother, I am ready to comfort you in times of trouble.

I open My arms and in a mother's tender voice coo, "There, there. It will be all right."

I love you with a Father's love, but I love with a Mother's love too.

Mountain

It was at the top of the mountain where Abraham put his full trust in Me.

It was at the top of the mountain where Moses answered My call.

The mountain top provides spectacular views after an arduous climb.

If you are facing a mountain of trouble and obstacles, put your full trust in Me.

I will help you climb the mountain, go around the mountain, or even move the mountain.

I am your Mountain Guide.

Music

Your life can be compared to music.

Music that is rich is not made up of one note but many.

In music there are high notes and there are low notes.

Music has its dissonance where notes clash with one another from time to time.

But they resolve back into harmony.

When you listen, life is a symphony of sounds.

All of My creation makes music.

There is the music of the rain and the ocean waves.

The birds and creatures sing their refrains to Me in praise.

Create beautiful harmony when you make music in your heart with Me.

Night

At night when you lay your head on your pillow, check in with Me before you say good night.

If a racing mind makes you toss and turn night after night, turn those thoughts over to Me.

Night is time for rest. The darkness is a reminder to stop and ease out of the day.

Each night know that I never sleep. I am watching over you. I am watching over all of creation.

Night does not last for long.

A new day awaits you full of hope, promise, and possibilities.

Persist

I made all of nature to persist, including you.

The eagle will persist in learning how to fly so that it will not only leave the nest, but soar above the clouds.

The tiny acorn will persist and grow into a massive oak tree, spreading its leaves upward toward heaven.

You were built to persist and grow. My creation weathers the elements and the storms because of persistence.

Persist in seeking My love and guidance.

I persist in showing you what great love I have for you.

Planted

I want you to be like a tree that is planted by a stream of water.

Its leaves never whither. It produces fruit and is prosperous.

You may not know who planted ideas in you – ideas that somehow you are inferior, unworthy, or not enough.

You must not let these false seeds planted, take root in you.

Don't be wooed by every opportunity that comes your way.

Sometimes you must stay where you are planted.

I have planted seeds of greatness within you.

Hear Me whisper in your ear, "Grow, grow, grow."

Presence

My presence is all around you.

The sun, moon, stars, and sky reflect My presence.

My presence is in every living thing.

In the beginning, I breathed life into Adam.

With each breath you take, be mindful of My presence within you.

When you are mindful of My presence, you will have presence of mind in times of trouble.

My loving presence will calm you and comfort you.

When busyness and overwhelm come your way, retreat to a quiet place and feel My presence.

My presence will keep stress and troubles at bay.

When you feel fearful or lost, My presence will shelter you and light your way.

River

When you let go and trust Me, your life will flow like a river.

A river has a definite course.

At times, there may be snags, obstacles, or rapids along the way.

But My love and guidance will help you to get unstuck to once again flow downstream.

My Spirit is your traveling companion.

You can drink from My river.

Its water is pure and will satisfy your thirst, your thirst for love, acceptance, belonging, and direction.

Trust Me.

Let My river of love carry you, sustain you, and guide you.

Salt

Salt is a very important ingredient.

Salt is used to preserve, cure, or treat.

Salt is also used to add flavor.

My Word is like salt.

It will preserve you, cure your wounded heart, and treat what ails you.

My Word is like salt, adding flavor and richness to your life.

But if salt loses its flavor, it becomes useless.

My salt never loses its flavor.

You are the salt of the earth.

Remain in My Word.

Be flavor-full.

Seasons

I have given you the seasons to help you remember that life is a cycle.

You crave certainty and security.

When challenges arise, remember the seasons.

Fall is a time to get ready. It is a time to plant prior to winter and spring. In some cases, the fall has produced a harvest that is stored for the winter ahead.

Winter is a time of rest. The work has been done and it's now a time of waiting.

Spring arrives with the promise of new life. The winter is past.

Summer comes producing the fruits from the fall and spring labor. Care is taken to nurture the garden and keep out the weeds.

The cycle continues back to fall.

Whatever season you are in, feel secure that there is always the harvest to look forward to when you have sown and nurtured the seed.

Shade

A tree provides needed shade from the hot sun. This shade comes as welcome relief.

But shade that turns to darkness must be stopped. Shade in this case blocks the light.

A shade of fear,

A shade of doubt,

A shade of worry, can plunge you into darkness.

My light will cast away this darkness.

When things heat up, you can rest in the shade of My loving presence to protect you and refresh you.

Shelter

I will provide shelter when life's elements threaten to harm you.

When the winds of change blow and knock you off your feet, I will provide a shelter to block the wind and help you regain your footing.

When stormy thoughts of fear and doubt pelt down on you, I will provide a shelter of peace to block those thoughts that threaten to drown you.

When a scorching sun beats down causing hope and dreams to dry up, I will provide a shelter with shade to shield your hopes and dreams so they can flourish and grow.

I am your sure and constant Shelter.

Sign

I give you a sign of faithfulness each day as the sun rises and sets.

The birds in the trees represent a sign that I care and provide for them.

Imagine how much more I love and provide for you.

All of My creation is a sign of My abundance and artistry.

When your spirit is disturbed, this is a warning sign to which you must pay attention.

I will provide you a sign of peace and clarity when you make decisions.

On your heart I sign an eternal, unbreakable commitment of My love for you.

Tree

I want you to be like a tree that will grow as tall as it can be. The winds and storms may blow, but you will be a tree to stand tall through it all.

Be like a tree that provides shade for others when heat threatens to consume.

Be like an oak tree whose roots are deep, rooted in My love and promises for you.

Wonder

Little children naturally have a sense of wonder. They have not become desensitized by the monotony or cynicism of daily life.

All things are new, and they are filled with wonder.

Wonder is one of My greatest gifts of joy to you.

Why do you think I paint a new sun rise and sunset for you each day?

Why do you think I created millions of stars and fish in the sea and flowers on the earth?

I want to remind you to always have My gift of wonder.

Wonder in how wondrous My love is for you.

Chapter 2

Body

When I created the earth and the heavens, I filled them with color and beauty. To each creature I gave a purpose, a part to play.

Each body is equipped to live out that purpose. Listen closely when I say that there is no ideal body. You strive to reach and maintain an ideal that is false. Have you ever thought that you worship and serve an ideal body? Is this not a form of idolatry?

The crowning touch to My masterpiece of creation was the creation of humankind. It saddens Me when you criticize your body or are ashamed of your body. It saddens Me when you compare your body to others and feel inferior.

It saddens Me when you don't use your body and move your body. Your body was created for movement and strength. When you don't care for your body, you can't live out your purpose with energy and gladness.

Your body is part of the collective body of the human race. It is your body; your hands, your feet, your heart, your voice, your mind, your actions that I use to carry My love physically into the world.

So, love your body. Nourish your body. Care for your body. Use your body.

Act

When you are inspired, act.

When you see injustice, act.

When you hear My voice inside of you, act.

When you make a decision, act.

When someone needs comfort, act.

When someone needs recognition, act.

Do not act in a rash or opposing manner.

My Spirit of truth, love, and compassion will act on your behalf when your actions are guided by Me.

Action

Your faith becomes tangible when you take action.

Take action when someone is hurting.

Take action when someone needs help.

Take action when life overwhelms you.

Any small action you do will restore your hope and confidence.

I take constant action on your behalf.

You may not see it, but My action is there, arranging, providing a way.

The biggest action you can take is putting your full trust in Me.

I will never fail you.

Awake

Awake! It is a new day, a new start!

Awake your senses. Awake your eyes, ears, and nose to the sights, sounds, and smells of everything around you.

Awake to awareness. Be fully present in each moment today.

Awake to mindfulness. Be mindful to treat yourself and others with loving kindness.

Awake from your sleep to the light of My loving presence to fuel your mind, body, and spirit for the day.

Awake.

Balance

Life will throw you off balance.

Recover your balance quickly when you steady yourself and hold onto Me.

Your life is like an investment account. The balance will grow in richness when the balance of your contributions are invested in love, kindness, and helping others.

Live out the balance of your life by looking to Me to lead you and guide you.

Body

I gave you a wonderful body that quietly functions, maintaining and sustaining your life.

It's important to take good care of your body, because it holds My Spirit.

Your body is a temple. Treat it like one.

Don't obsess about your body, what you will eat, what you will wear, your outward appearance, and comparing yourself to others. This preoccupation with the body causes unneeded suffering.

The body is temporary. The spirit is eternal.

When you nurture your spirit, the body will receive what it needs.

Breathe

To breathe is to be alive.

Stop and take in several deep breaths throughout the day. This is taking a breather to refresh your soul.

Imagine you are breathing in My loving presence to fill you with peace and clarity for your day.

Breathe in the sights and sounds of nature.

Breathe in the sounds of children's voices and the voices of those you love.

Breathe.

Call

Nature will call you when your spirit needs beauty.

Sleep will call you when your body needs rest.

Your heart will call you when you get too busy.

Your mind will call you to take a break.

Friends call you to connect and to share.

I call you to remember My love for you.

You can call on Me anytime, anywhere and I will be there for you.

Eyes

Life moves fast like the twinkling of an eye.

That's why you must keep your eyes open.

Have eyes for those in need.

Have eyes for opportunities.

Have eyes to see people's hearts and souls, not just outward appearances.

When you see others through My eyes, you will be filled with love, compassion, and understanding.

I wish you could fully comprehend what glory I see in you, if you could only look through My eyes.

Face

When you look in the mirror and see your face today, know that your image is My image.

I created you in My image.

You are My beloved child. So, you can:

Face the world with confidence.

Face any challenges that come your way.

Face the day with gratitude and gladness.

My face shines upon you as you face each moment of each new day.

Feel

Feel My presence within you.

You can feel it when you are conscious of your breath.

When you breathe, think of breathing in My presence.

I want you to feel loved and secure.

If you must:

> Feel guilt,
> Feel doubt,
> Feel fear,
> Feel inadequate.

Feel all those emotions, but let them go quickly.

You may not feel like letting go.

But you must let go in order to feel up to fulfilling the wonderful plans I have for you.

Feelings

Feelings are part of the senses I gave you like: sight, hearing, touch, taste, and smell.

Feelings of fear can be crucial to your survival, or, feelings of fear can be unfounded.

Feelings of sadness are part of life and loss. They will not last for long.

Feelings will help you make a difficult decision when you've weighed all the facts.

Feelings express the soul's aliveness.

To feel feelings of love and compassion is the richest of all gifts.

I want you to bask in feelings of total love and security.

You are My beloved.

My feelings for you will never change.

Hand

Sometimes you may think you have been dealt a bad hand and that life is stacked against you.

You will feel this way when you let go of My hand.

You have a hand in many choices that can cause hardships in your life.

On the other hand, there are circumstances that are not of your choosing.

When you hand over your cares, burdens, and worries, I will give you the strength to deal with what is at hand.

I will offer you a hand in times of trouble.

Take My hand. I will never let it go.

Hear

Hear the sound of your breath as you sit here with Me. Hear your heart beating. It is a reminder that your body is quietly supporting you.

Stop to:

Hear the wind in the trees.

Hear the songs of the birds.

Hear the feet of your children padding down the hall.

Hear the nightly symphony of crickets and bull frogs.

Hear the sounds of the city, people working to provide for others, themselves, and their families.

Hear My voice telling you; you are unique and powerful beyond measure.

Never forget how much I love you ... hear?

Heart

G uard your heart because it is the wellspring of life. But don't be guarded. If you have been hurt, don't allow this hurt to shut off your heart.

If you do, you will not receive all the blessings I have for you.

Have an open heart, but only allow those in who are wholehearted.

That means you must be wholehearted too, whole, loving, and living with the highest integrity.

Live life with your whole heart.

Take heart.

Have heart.

Know that I love you with all of My heart.

Human

I created you as a human in My image.

Jesus took on human form, a life filled with joy, love, pain, and suffering.

And, like Jesus, I have given you My Spirit.

I feel your joy, love, pain, and suffering.

My Spirit is written on your human heart.

You were born human, but seeking My Spirit of truth, you are born anew, into Spirit.

Your human wisdom thus expands to spiritual wisdom.

No human eye can see, nor human ear hear, nor human heart conceive, what I have prepared for those who love Me.

Laugh

There's a time to weep and a time to laugh.

I want you to laugh more often.

When you laugh, it lightens your spirit.

When you laugh, you forget your troubles.

However, when I present you with a grand idea or mission, why do you laugh?

Abraham's wife Sarah laughed when I told her she would have a son in her old age.

Despite giving a laugh, Sarah put her trust in Me.

I made the impossible come true. She had a son and named him Isaac, which means laughter.

I am the God of surprises.

I love to make you laugh.

Listen

Listen to your life. It is speaking to you when you listen.

Listen with your heart, and not only with your ears.

Listen to My Spirit within you. It speaks the truth.

Listen to your body. It speaks to you when its tired or depleted. Don't ignore it. Listen.

Listen to those who are speaking to you. Give them your full attention. Hear what they are really saying.

When you call on Me, I listen.

Be wise.

Stop talking.

Listen.

Observe

To observe is greater than seeing. Learn to observe situations throughout your day.

To observe is to see, but to see something as a whole and from a nonjudgmental distance.

In a meeting, observe the conversation and don't speak.

Listen and observe posture, tone of voice, gestures.

When you are in nature, truly observe all that is around you.

Pay close attention, and you will observe things you've never seen before.

Observe the Sabbath. It is good to rest one day. I do.

Observe and truly see the wonderful world and all that is within, which I've created for you.

Protect

Your instincts and intuition will protect you from disaster when you listen.

I can't protect you from a broken heart, but I can heal it.

If you avoid risk in loving others and letting others love you, you may protect yourself from heartache, but you won't fully live.

Associating with others who are honorable will protect you from trouble.

Being authentic in your words and actions will protect you from anxiety and conflict.

I am here to protect you and guide you always.

Rest

The world calls you to be busy, but I call you to rest.

Rest your mind from doubt, worries, and troubles.

Rest your body with sleep.

Rest in the arms of My comfort.

Rest in the shelter of My protection.

Rest assured that I am with you and will love you always.

Safety

Y ou seek safety in a job, relationship, or finances.

Beware of constantly seeking safety outwardly.

You want freedom and freedom from risk.

But if you never risk, you will never grow.

Freedom comes from letting go of safety.

When you trust in Me, I will provide safety from the storms that come.

I will supply your every need.

Seek Me.

In Me you will find safety.

See

You think you cannot see Me, but I am here.

You see Me in the eyes of your loved ones.

You see Me in the vastness of creation.

You see My work through compassionate help and support given to you.

You see My love through answered prayer.

Trust in Me and I will see you through life's journey.

Self-control

I have given you My Spirit, but I've also given you free will.

That's why you must use self-control.

Use self-control when faced with gossip, lest you hurt another.

Use self-control in your eating and drinking, lest you harm your body.

Use self-control when someone provokes you, lest you stoop to their level.

Use self-control and moderation in all things, lest you be knocked off balance.

Self-control leads to discipline, patience, knowledge, endurance, and love.

Practice self-control and your life will be fruitful.

Sleep

Sleep is necessary to refresh the body.

Your sleep will be peaceful when you have a clear conscience.

Whatever is troubling you make it right tomorrow.

Your sleep will be fitful when you are anxious and worried.

Turn your anxiety and worry over to Me.

Don't rush to make decisions.

Sleep on it.

Don't sleep during the day.

You need to keep awake.

Pay attention.

Be present.

Too many people sleepwalk through life.

I want your sleep to be peaceful.

Then you will be refreshed to face a new day.

Smile

A smile is such a simple gesture, but its effect can change someone's day.

Smile at the bank teller, cashier, or the person serving your food.

Smile at someone who has a disability.

A smile is a loving connection.

It acknowledges to the other person and says, "I see you. You and I are connected. We are in this together. We are part of God's family."

As a loving parent smiles as they are watching over their infant sleeping, I smile over you.

Step

Life's journey is taken one step at a time.

Consistent growth and grand opportunities rarely come from taking great leaps.

As a toddler, your first mark of independence came when you took your first step.

When Moses delivered the Israelites away from their Egyptian captors, their freedom came when

they took the first step off of dry land, as the Red Sea parted before their eyes.

Having a happy, joy-filled, peaceful, fulfilling life comes as a result of taking small steps each day.

Stay in step with Me, and I will lead you and guide you in the direction you wish to go.

Strength

Strength isn't purely brawn or muscles.

Strength is much greater than that.

When you harness My strength, I give you strength to emerge through any challenge or hardship.

I give you strength to speak the truth and to stand up for yourself and others.

I give you strength to face each day with confidence, My confidence within you.

Accept My strength.

Use My strength for good.

Try

You don't have to try to find Me, I'm right here.

Contrary to what you may think, you never try My patience.

Don't try to please everyone. You will feel empty, not full.

I am sad when you try so hard on your own.

I am your strength so that you don't need to try so hard.

Trying to make things happen will leave you exhausted.

Allow Me to work through you.

Trust Me.

Give allowing a try.

Voice

When you are attentive, you will hear My voice.

My voice speaks to you through yearnings.

My voice speaks to you on the wind.

My voice speaks to you through intuition.

My voice speaks to you through My creation.

My voice speaks to you through a song, an idea, a suggestion made to you.

Voice your cares, concerns, joys, and sorrows to Me.

My voice will even speak through you when you listen to Me.

Walk

Walk in my ways.

Walk in truth.

Walk in understanding.

Walk in patience.

Walk with a purpose.

Walk humbly.

Walk with your eyes fully open, not in blindness.

Walk out of your darkness into the light.

Listen very closely and you will hear My voice whisper behind you, "Walk this way."

Chapter 3

Mind

When I created you, I gave you a complex mind. Your mind can process a lot of information. It is able to store a lot of knowledge and memories. This can be good and this can be bad.

It's good when you can use that knowledge that you retain. It will help you in many areas of your life and in making good decisions.

It can be bad when you allow your mind to be overwhelmed with thoughts of fear, doubts, anger, or regrets. Holding onto mistakes, holding on to the past, can give you a mind that is not at peace. It will stunt your growth. So, you must clear those limiting, fearful thoughts from your mind.

Your mind has the power to expand when you feed it. Be careful what you feed your mind, because it affects your spirit, My Spirit within you.

I made you in My image. As Creator, I have made *you* a creator. I am amazed at how far humans have come in such a short time using their minds to create. Each day technology keeps evolving. However, I did not create the mind to absorb so much information so quickly. It is overwhelming to the mind.

Don't over expose yourself to negativity and violence. It will disturb your mind and spirit. Instead, expose your mind to what is good and honorable and loving.

Give your mind a rest. It needs downtime to recharge and to think clearly.

Don't close off your mind. Keep your mind open to new concepts, ideas, and opportunities to help you grow and renew your mind.

Above all, when your mind is focused on Me, you will know peace, power, and contentment.

Center

Center your thoughts on Me and I will bring you peace.

When you make Me the center of your world, that's when you can harness all of My power to go to work for you.

My Spirit dwells in the center of your heart.

My loving life force will center you, and keep you grounded.

Choice

Every day you have a choice to create a beautiful day and a beautiful future.

Say, "I have a choice."

Choose wisely.

Your good choices today determine your future.

Your good choices will bless you, and you will be a blessing to others.

It's your choice.

Make a choice to have a grateful heart.

Make a choice to be kind to yourself and others.

Make a choice to eat well, exercise, and get enough rest so that you can serve the world effectively.

Make a choice to listen and pay attention to friends and loved ones.

I created you with divine love.

I do not choose what you will do.

My unconditional love gives you the freedom of choice.

Clear

I can see right through you.

So, there is no use hiding anything from Me.

I will clear your guilt or shame and give you love.

I will clear your anxiety or fear and give you peace.

I will take away your confusion and cloudiness and make things clear.

When you take time to be still and listen, My voice becomes clear.

When you have a clear conscience, you will also be clear-minded.

I will make clear to you which path to take and clear obstacles out of your way.

Content

Your heart, mind, and spirit are restless because you are not content.

Instead, you may become contentious, stressing and striving for more and more. Never satisfied.

Are you really content with that?

Your world wants you to believe that being content is being lazy or settling for second best.

Until you learn to be content, you won't be at peace.

A contented heart is a grateful heart.

Know that I supply your every need.

In fact, I will supply all of your heart's content when you let go and trust in Me.

Create

I did not create you to feel constant fear or lack.

Come to Me with your concerns, and I will create a renewed spirit within you.

I have given you a brilliant mind so that you can create.

I have given you an amazing body to create movement through dance and athletics and accomplishing physical tasks.

My will is that you create the life you want that will use your gifts and talents to the fullest.

I am the great Creator. I am in you.

Together we will create a life well lived.

Empty

Empty your worries and cares. Let them spill out onto the ground and be blown away by the wind.

Empty your mind of swirling, stressful, anxious thoughts of to-do lists and demands.

I will fill your mind with peace.

Empty your heart of concerns or heartache.

I will fill it with love and appreciation.

When you empty yourself to Me, I fill you with peace, love, joy, and grace to face your day.

Enough

Be careful and do not listen to the outside voices of your culture that promote scarcity and its manufactured model of perfectionism. These voices say you're not:

Good enough,
Smart enough,
Rich enough,
Young enough,
Old enough,
Pretty enough,
Handsome enough,
Skinny enough ...
Enough!

When you listen to the outside voices, you drown out the voice of Truth. You drown out the only voice that matters. It's the still small voice that I gave you. It is My voice that whispers to you.

You are strong enough,
You are smart enough,
You are enough.

Examine

E xamine the words and actions of others to see if they are true.

Examine your own life before you give advice.

When you ask Me for anything, I examine your true intentions.

When you examine your heart and motives, you can make sincere requests of Me.

Imagine

Imagine what your life would be like if you had no fear or doubts.

Imagine trusting in Me to open doors of opportunity.

Imagine what it feels like to be loved completely and unconditionally no matter what you have done wrong.

Imagine letting go of the burden of the past in the form of mistakes, errors in judgment, or words

said that caused the loss of relationships.

Imagine your life unfolding, fulfilling dreams, and experiencing joy.

When you put your trust in Me, what you imagine, I will help you bring forth.

Keep

Hear My voice whisper to you:

Keep dreaming.

Keep trusting.

Keep loving.

Keep hoping.

Keep trying.

Keep learning.

Keep your mind focused on Me and I will keep you in perfect peace.

Key

The key to peace is to still your mind from racing thoughts. Set your mind on Me.

The key to joy is to let go of your burdens, hurts, or the past. Give them to Me.

The key to success is listening to what makes your heart sing. Then trust in My strength and power. I will guide you and open doors for you.

The key to abundance is coming to Me for provision. I am your unlimited Source, your Supreme Provider.

The key to be loved is to be loving.

When life feels off key, come to Me and I'll restore harmony.

You are a treasure!

I hold the key to unlocking the glory inside of you.

Lack

When you rest in Me, you will lack nothing.

Seek Me when you lack understanding. I will grant it.

Seek Me when you lack peace. You will find it.

Seek Me when you lack financially. I will provide.

Never focus on lack.

I gave you a powerful mind to create.

When you focus on lack, you will create lack in your life.

Focus on gratitude and your thoughts of lack will turn to abundance.

Those who seek Me lack for nothing.

Learn

L earn from Me. I am your Purveyor of Truth.

Learn to do right.

Learn to listen.

Learn to forgive.

Learn to love.

Learn to let go of the past.

Learn to forget things you were taught about Me, yourself, or others that are not true.

Learn to rest from your striving.

Learn to trust Me.

Learn from Me.

Meditate

Think on, plan on, meditate on what is true.

Meditate on love.

Meditate on hope.

Meditate on peace.

Meditate on My loving presence within you and within the world.

When you meditate on these words, you will receive peace, love, clarity, and direction.

Mind

A mind not at rest will make you restless.

A racing mind will keep you from peace.

A cluttered mind will cause stress and cause you to make poor decisions.

That's because you can't make up your mind.

When your mind is on worries, you will lose your mind.

Make up your mind to take your focus off earthly things and concerns.

I will keep your mind in perfect peace when you focus your mind on Me.

Mindful

Each day I want you to be mindful.

Be mindful of your tone of voice – how you speak and treat others, and how you speak and treat yourself.

Be mindful of how you spend your time.

Make each day meaningful.

Be mindful of your actions.

Others are watching.

Be mindful of the earth and all of creation. I gave you dominion over it to care for it.

Never forget that I am mindful of your going out and coming in.

I am mindful of all your needs.

Narrow

I ask you to walk a narrow road.

The road will require taking a path inward.

Narrow does not mean dangerous.

Narrow can mean difficult.

A narrow path requires focus.

You are easily distracted by the outside voices of fame, fortune, and recognition.

This can force you to lose your way from time to time.

Don't be narrow-minded.

Judgments weigh you down.

The narrow road requires that you travel lightly.

That means not being narrow-minded in believing what is possible.

With Me *all* things are possible.

Trust in Me and I will keep you on the straight and narrow road to joy, abundance, and freedom.

Nourishment

Nourishment is more than food for the body.
First and foremost, your body is a temple.
Seek good nourishment to take care of your body.

Seek nourishment for your mind.

Feed your mind with My Word, follow other spiritual teachers, and consume other healthy spiritual food.

Be informed in the world, but don't be inundated.

You will become drained and depleted.

Seek nourishment for your soul through silence and being in My presence.

This type of nourishment will bring you peace, health, and happiness.

Open

Open your mind.

Open your heart.

Open yourself to Me.

When you are open, you are able to receive My blessings.

Open your mind and heart to others. When you do, I will open doors of others' hearts closed off to you.

I will open doors of opportunities for you.

Open your eyes to see how I've loved and protected you and will continue to.

Come to Me with your joys and sorrows. My door is always open.

Peace

I want you to experience My peace.

Don't try to understand My peace, just embrace it.

Peace cannot exist when war is going on.

Your mind will be at war with peace when it's filled with thoughts that attack your abilities, worthiness, or pass judgments.

Your life will be at war with peace when it's burdened with the stress of too many commitments, work that consumes and depletes you, stress caused by compromising your values, and not caring for your health and well-being.

Be at peace.

Stop what you are doing, close your eyes, and breathe in My peace.

When you begin to feel like you are under siege, stop.

Let My peace fill your entire being from head to toe, bathing you in love and lightness.

Remember

Remember stories of those who have gone before you. They are a testimony to My love and faithfulness.

Remember those who are hurting.

Remember those who are lonely.

Remember those who are hungry.

Remember those in need. There are many.

Remember that there is something you can do for them, even just to pray.

Remember your blessings.

Remember to say thank you.

Remember My promises that I will always love you and never leave you.

Remind

Let Me remind you Whose you are. You are My precious child.

Let Me remind you, that makes you an heir to My Kingdom.

Let Me remind you that you were created with perfect love and not with fear.

Let Me remind you that you are a child of light.

Where there is light, there can be no darkness.

Let Me remind you that you are never alone, I am always with you.

Let Me remind you that with Me, all things are possible.

Set

Set aside your worries and cares as you spend this time with Me.

Get set for all the wonderful plans I have in store for you.

My plans invoke your plans as you set worthy goals and set your intentions, asking for My strength and direction to carry them out.

You may have setbacks, but they are only temporary, and usually necessary course corrections.

When you set your mind on Me, I will set your mind, heart, and spirit free.

Share

Stop thinking about getting your fair share.

In My world, source is unlimited!

I share with you My abundance.

I share with you My joy.

I share with you My peace.

I share with you My wisdom.

I share with you My creativity.

I share with you My power.

This is not a one-way street.

Know that I share in your joys.

I share in your sorrows.

We share our lives together.

Share all of what I've given you with others.

Should

You become stressed and anxious when your mind runs on with thinking, should I do this, or should I do that?

What you *should* do is come to Me for guidance. I will make decisions clear and give you peace.

Should you be surprised when your health fails, when you should have taken better care of the body and mind which I gave you to care for?

You should not wallow in guilt or self-reproach.

It is unproductive energy.

Instead, you should forgive and make amends quickly.

Should you have any doubt, know that I love you no matter what.

Should you stumble, I am here to catch you before you fall.

Simply

Y ou cause stress and feel overwhelmed when you don't handle things simply.

Simply say yes or no when asked.

No explanation is needed.

Simply silence your racing thoughts by stopping and taking a few deep breaths.

Breathe in My loving, peaceful presence.

Eliminate resentment and anger when you stop judging others or yourself.

Simply stop.

Acquiring and caring for too many possessions causes clutter and stress.

Clear space.

Live simply.

Simply turn your worries and cares over to Me.

I will provide you with peace, joy, and lightness.

Space

I want you to create and enjoy gracious space.

Clear your cluttered thoughts and make space for clarity.

Clear your anxious thoughts and make space for peace.

When someone is aggressive towards you, don't react with aggression.

Allow space between you to respond in a thoughtful way.

Create space in your surroundings.

Space helps you to feel open and expansive.

Don't crowd out My presence with doubts and fears.

Leave space in your mind, heart, and spirit for Me to dwell.

Still

Still your anxious thoughts.

Still your hurried pace, and rest in Me.

Still your judgments over mistakes you've made or doubts that you have.

I still love you, no matter what.

I will still the judgments, doubts, and anxious thoughts when you turn them over to me.

Be still and know that I am God.

Stop

When anxious thoughts fill your mind and spirit, stop, and turn to Me.

I will keep you in perfect peace when you keep your mind on Me.

When you're feeling confused or overwhelmed, stop, take a deep breath.

Remember that I am not the author of confusion, but of peace.

When you have decisions to make, stop, take a deep breath.

Listen for My guidance and direction.

When you stop and be still in My presence, I will stop your anxiety and confusion and help you start anew.

There

You are always trying to get there.

But when you are there, you can't stop thinking about being somewhere else.

There! Now you see how crazy that thinking is?

There are blessings you will miss when you don't live in the here and now.

There is love here.

There is beauty here.

There is joy here.

There is peace here.

There is significance here.

I whisper to you, "there, there."

Stop your racing thoughts and actions.

There you will find rest.

Think

Don't over think things.

Instead, think on My promises to you:

Nothing is impossible with Me,

I will never leave you,

I love you with an everlasting love.

Think on what is true.

Think on what is lovely.

Think on what is just.

When you do, you will feel My loving peace within you.

Thoughts

You create with thoughts.

Have thoughts of fear and you will create fear.

Have thoughts of stress and you will create stress.

Have thoughts of being overwhelmed and you will create overwhelm.

Have thoughts of love and you will create love.

Have thoughts of kindness and you will create kindness.

Have thoughts of peace and you will create peace.

I know all of your thoughts.

Let My loving presence be at the top of your thoughts.

Then you will create a beautiful life guided by Me.

Vision

I have a great vision for you.

It is to live out your life with peace, love, clarity, and boldness!

But I can't make this vision happen.

You must share the vision.

You must see this vision,

Embrace this vision,

Execute this vision.

This vision is simply the desires of your heart manifesting each day.

That is My vision for you.

Wisdom

If you feel you lack wisdom, ask and it shall be given.

In Me are the hidden treasures of understanding, knowledge, and wisdom.

True wisdom is expressed through humility.

My Spirit of wisdom is within you.

You manifest My wisdom through your actions.

My Word and wisdom are true.

I pass My wisdom onto you.

Words

Words can inspire and words can destroy.

Kind words will lift your spirit.

Encouraging words will move you forward.

Inspiring words will give you hope.

Harsh words will shut you down.

Critical words will thwart your forward progress and crush your hope.

Words are very powerful.

Be careful how you use them.

Above all, be careful whose words you listen to.

Heed My words, you are one of a kind and precious to Me beyond measure.

Listen to these words and take them to heart, because My words are true.

Worthy

My greatest sorrow rests in seeing My children feel that they are not worthy.

Oh, the accomplishments and great things that you are so worthy and capable of doing if you only believed it!

You listen to the earthly voices of those who have no authority to tell you that you are not worthy. You think they have authority.

Those who tell you that you are unworthy may be a parent, a manager, or teacher.

I am the Ultimate Authority.

I am the Author of all things.

I am the Creator of you.

There is no one else like you.

You are precious and priceless to Me.

Know that you are worthy beyond measure.

Chapter 4

Spirit

In the beginning, My Spirit moved across the waters. My Spirit creates. My Spirit gives life. My Spirit holds great power. This same power is within you. That makes *you* creative and powerful.

Many never realize this truth. They are caught up in a material world focused on striving and acquiring. They are searching for fulfillment and peace outside of themselves: the next diet, the next anti-aging product, the next promotion, more education, the next brighter, bigger, better purchase. The search is never enough. There is always the desire for more.

Okay, I confess, I created you with a longing and yearning. That's because I want you to love Me as much as I love you.

When you accept My love and Spirit within you, you will no longer have those yearnings for more in the material world. You will cross over into My world, the world of Spirit.

I have not given you a spirit of fear, but of power and love. My Spirit will ease your troubled mind in a troubled world.

Through My Spirit I am your Companion, always with you, whispering words of guidance and encouragement.

You may not see Me, but you will see My Spirit working for you on your behalf. You'll feel My Spirit through peace, discernment, and contentment.

My Spirit is strong within you.

Abide

Abide in Me and I abide in you.

Abide in the shelter of My love.

Abide in the sanctuary of My peace.

Abide in knowing that you are enough.

There is no need to constantly strive and achieve.

Accept the blessings of life right here, right now, when you abide in Me.

Able

I have given you My Spirit. My loving, powerful Spirit is all around you and within you.

It whispers the words gently into your ear; you are able.

You are able to make it through this day.

You are able to make it through this moment.

You are able to forgive the unforgivable.

You are able to love the unlovable.

You are able to do the impossible.

You are able.

All

You may feel all alone, but I am always with you.

I share in all of your suffering.

I share in all of your joy.

When you trust Me, when you are all in, you love Me with:

All of your heart,

All of your soul,

And all of your mind.

You don't have to do things all by yourself.

I tell you all the more, with Me all things are possible.

Angels

Angels are My messengers.

Angels came to Abraham and to Sarah to tell them that they would have a son.

An angel came to Mary to tell her that she would have a son named Jesus.

Angels came to the tomb to tell Mary Magdalene that Jesus was not there.

The first message angels deliver is, "Fear not."

Angels are My way of getting someone's complete attention.

Angels are all around you.

Angels come in human form and animal form.

Angels protect you and guide you.

Listen. Watch. Sense.

Is it a soft breeze, or is the air brushing across your face the movement of an angel's wings?

Bold

I don't wish for you to live your life being timid.

No! I want you to be bold!

Be bold in your speech.

Be bold in your actions.

I have not given you a spirit of fear but of confidence and boldness.

Bold does not mean flashy.

Bold does not mean abrupt or rude.

To be bold is to speak the truth.

Take bold action, and stand up for yourself and others.

Be bold like a lion, taking hold of My strength and power.

Breath

Breath is life.

Man did not live until I breathed into him his first breath.

My breath, My Spirit is within you.

When you are stressed, stop, take a deep breath.

With each breath you breathe in the awareness of My peaceful, loving, powerful presence.

Close

Pay close attention.

When the world begins to close in on you, call on Me.

I am always close by.

I will still your racing heart when you have a close call or sense fear or danger.

Keep Me close to your heart.

I hold you close and will never let you go.

Color

I love color!

Just look at the color of each flower, the color of each bird, the color of the sea and all that lives therein.

Look at the color of your skin.

Color is beauty.

Don't let someone color your opinion without first seeking the truth.

I created you to be creative just like Me.

Express yourself with color.

Show your true colors.

Allow Me to color your world with joy and beauty.

Compassion

Like any good parent, I have compassion for My children. When you suffer, I suffer. I long for people to have compassion for one another.

But the world I once created out of My love and compassion is full of pain.

Until you feel another person's pain, you will not understand the meaning of true compassion.

When one part of the body suffers, it affects the whole body.

When one of My children suffers, humanity suffers.

My Spirit of compassion is within you.

Share compassion with others.

Day

It is a new day!

What will you face this day?

Is it a typical workday?

Feel My presence this day to lighten your spirit.

Do you face a challenge this day?

Feel My presence giving you strength and guidance.

Do you need to rest this day?

Then rest, let go of feeling guilt or sadness. Rest this day.

Are you bored this day?

Find someone in need that you can help or encourage.

Make the most of this day.

Day in and day out, think of Me.

At the end of the day, tell Me about it.

Above all, give thanks for *this* day and *every* day.

Desire

I desire only the best for you.

I desire that you be happy.

I desire that you feel fulfilled.

I desire that you let go of feelings of unworthiness, because you are a treasure.

I desire that you let go of fear and trust Me to give you peace and clarity.

Express your desires to Me.

When what you desire is true, I will give you the desires of your heart.

Equipped

I have equipped you with all that you need to perform good in the world.

I have equipped you with a brilliant mind.

I have equipped you with an able body.

I have equipped you with My loving Spirit.

I have equipped you with My power.

When your mind or body should fail or become frail, My strong Spirit and ceaseless love will sustain you.

I have equipped your spirit to be resilient.

I will equip you with strength when you rely on Me.

Ever

Have you ever thought that there would never, ever be anyone just like you?

Before you were ever born, I knew about you, planned for you.

Have you ever really fathomed how much I love you?

If there's ever any fear or doubt that creeps into your mind, let it go and ever lean on Me.

Be ever seeing so that you can perceive.

Be ever hearing so that you can listen and understand.

Whenever you need Me, I am here.

Know that My love for you will last forever and ever.

Everlasting

L ife in the material world is temporal.

If you focus on striving and accumulating possessions, these goals and things are fleeting.

Living in My realm is everlasting. There you'll find:

Everlasting peace,

Everlasting love,

Everlasting joy,

I give you life everlasting right now and forever.

Fabric

Your life is a fabric, a tapestry woven together with experiences and relationships.

The front of the fabric will be beautiful and colorful.

The back of the fabric, however, may look quite different.

It is full of knotted, twisted threads.

These threads represent the trials and triumphs that make up everyday life.

Each thread creates the fabric.

When you weave your fabric with the threads of joy, forgiveness, love and laughter, it will become a beautiful masterpiece.

My creation is one huge tapestry of many fabrics woven together.

If you were to see this fabric through My eyes, you would see a world united and at peace.

Forever

Forever means never-ending.

But it also means forever living in the present moment.

My love for you is forever.

My patience for you is forever.

My confidence in you is forever.

You can trust in Me forever.

I am your Rock and Shelter

My Spirit of love, truth, and power resides in you now and forever.

Gracious

I am Gracious and Compassionate.

Because My Spirit is within you, you are to be gracious and compassionate too.

Create gracious space in your life.

That means creating gracious space in your mind, gracious space in your surroundings, and gracious space in your heart.

This space allows you to cultivate peace and to receive My gracious favor and blessings.

Here

Come here. I want you to know:

I am right here, right now.

I am always here. You may not be aware of that.

I am here anytime of the day or night.

My peace, power, and joy are gifts offered to you. Here, take them.

Never forget that wherever you go, I am here, always present.

Hold

Hold onto My hand, I will never let you go.

Hold your complaining.

Focusing on fear, worry, or anxious thoughts will have a negative hold on you.

Instead, hold onto My promises:

I am not the author of confusion, but of peace.

I will never leave you or forsake you.

Nothing can separate My love from you.

These truths you can hold onto.

Holy

It is written: *be holy because I am holy.*

You are My child.

I have given you My Holy Spirit. Therefore, be:

Holy in your relationships,

Holy in your love,

Holy in all that you do.

You are My beloved.

My holy mountain is a place full of peace and spectacular views.

Stay close to Me holy one, and I will help you see all that I see for you.

Humble

I want you to be humble.

That does not mean being weak or submissive.

It means wiping out arrogance and pride in the form of superiority.

One of My greatest leaders, Moses, was a humble man.

My Son was born into humble surroundings.

He possessed a humble servant's heart, yet He was able to perform powerful miracles.

Many saints lived humble lives, yet their humility is remembered as greatness.

A humble spirit is a beautiful spirit.

What I require of you is very simple: seek to be just and fair, love kindness, walk humbly with Me.

Hungry

I satisfy the hungry heart.

If you are hungry for peace, I will calm your restless mind and spirit.

If you are hungry for approval, know how much I approve of you right at this moment.

My approval is all that you need.

Be hungry for knowledge, hungry to help others.

Too many people go hungry. Feed them.

If you are hungry for love, I will fill you with love that is overflowing.

I am hungry to fulfill all of your needs.

Inside

Happiness, peace, purpose, and fulfillment come to you not from outside of you, but from inside of you.

Inside you may long for acceptance, recognition, and love.

But you look outside to others to give you this validation.

You listen to the voices of the material world that tell you what you need to have, how to look, and to be.

When you look outside of yourself, you feel conflict on the inside.

I created you with a divine, perfect love.

When you fully understand that, you grasp that wholeness, peace, happiness, purpose, and fulfillment come from within.

I recognize you as a beautiful, powerful child of Mine.

When you know that, you will blossom from inside and search outside no more.

Invisible

My presence may be invisible to the eye, but I am here with you, watching over you.

Life's most precious treasures are invisible.

Love is invisible, but it becomes visible through actions of compassion and kindness.

Hope is invisible, but it shows up in someone lending a helping hand.

Faith is invisible, but it manifests in answered prayers and courage to keep going.

I no longer was invisible when I sent My Son as My visible, loving presence.

You are an expression of My image in the world, too.

Embrace the invisible, and you will see more clearly.

Invite

Invite Me with you as you go about your day.

Invite the sights, sounds, and beauty of nature into your senses to feel connected with everything around you.

Invite My peace to fill your spirit.

Invite My strength and love to sustain you.

I invite you to share a life with Me filled with peace, hope, and promise.

It is an endless invitation.

Judge

People will judge you by your religion or beliefs.

They will judge you by your appearance.

They will judge you by your speech.

They will judge you by your actions.

Even worse, *you* will judge *your* every action;

Judge your own decisions,

Judge your appearance,

And judge your abilities.

You may think that I judge your every move.

I am not the great judge.

You, on the other hand, have become quite an expert!

Stop being a judge.

You are precious, one-of-a-kind, whole, beautiful, and powerful beyond measure.

If I had a verdict, that is My final one.

Kind

You are one of a kind, unique, and precious.

You are not kind of like Me.

You are made in My image to exude power, creativity, peace, love, joy, gentleness, patience, and kindness.

When you are kind to yourself and kind to others, you show both of our true characters.

In all that you do, love, speak the truth, but above all, be kind.

Let

L et down your guard around Me.

Let Me hear about what is going on in your life.

That may mean you need to let off steam in the form of anger or sorrow.

Let it go, so you can let it be.

Let no one disturb you.

When you listen to others, let your words be few.

Let up on yourself. I don't judge you. So, why do you feel the constant need to?

Let not your heart be troubled, neither let it be afraid.

Above all else, let Me love you and remind you that all is well when you rest in Me.

Look

Look to Me and I will guide your steps.

Look around and appreciate the wonders of creation.

Look towards a life full of joy and abundance when you trust in Me.

Don't look down upon others.

Look for the good in others.

Look out for people wanting to steer you wrong.

Look inside of you for the truth.

Know that I look after you.

It is My greatest delight when you look to *Me*.

Meaning

Whatever you have been meaning to do, do it. Do not put it off; for you do not know if or when an opportunity will arise again.

Don't live your life without meaning.

There is meaning in relationships.

There is meaning in My creation through the expression of My love and beauty.

There is meaning in the dreams that you have.

I speak to you through the depths of your spirit.

Embrace My loving presence and I will fill your world with joy, wonder, and meaning.

Most

Most people are unconscious.

They go about most of their day going through the motions.

They aren't aware of My loving presence around them and within them.

At the most, they may say a brief prayer before meals or before bed.

You are not like most.

You are conscious and aware.

You see what I see in others, what is most beautiful, most promising.

Focus on what is most important today and every day.

I will provide you with endless opportunities.

Make the most of them.

Mystery

To embrace My love for you and your love for Me means to embrace mystery.

Who can explain it?

You can't see Me, yet here you are, wanting to hear what word I have for you today.

Your faith makes Me smile.

Who can explain how two small cells produce a life?

Who can explain how it is possible to think of someone you haven't seen in a long time, and suddenly that person contacts you?

The answer is mystery.

Walking with My Spirit means embracing mystery.

I am attentive to your heart's desires.

As you continue to trust in Me, mystery will unfold.

You will receive revelations as you connect the mysterious dots.

Now

I am with you now and always.

When you focus on the here and now, you will make the most of the present moment.

The past is gone. The future is yet to come.

What you do *now* will create your future.

Now is your time to shine.

Now is your time to break any obstacles.

Now hear this; I love and believe in you, now and always.

Pray

Pray for peace.

Pray for strength.

Pray for patience.

Pray for loved ones.

Pray for strangers.

Pray for your enemies and for those in danger.

Pray for understanding.

Pray for compassion.

Pray for the sick.

Pray for the lonely.

Pray for others and not you only.

Quiet

I n quiet moments, you can create an oasis of peace.

Quiet your mind.

Quiet your heart.

Quiet your body by taking deep breaths, breathing in My presence to quiet your anxiety.

When you become quiet, you can hear My whispers of love, encouragement, and guidance.

This instills My quiet confidence within you to face each day.

Receive

Y ou must be willing to accept in order to receive.

Receive My love.

Receive My mercy.

Receive My favor.

Receive My protection.

Receive My guidance.

Receive the talents I've given you. Explore them. Use them.

Receive My Spirit and power within you. Use it for good.

Ask for anything in My name and you will receive, but only if you trust and believe.

Recognize

You may wonder sometimes if I am paying attention to you.

Or, you may pay no attention to Me on some days.

I recognize all that you do.

It is not in a judging way.

I recognize your triumphs and I recognize your struggles.

People will recognize My Spirit within you by your actions.

They will recognize love, compassion, and kindness.

You will recognize My Spirit within you when you feel and exude love, peace, patience, generosity, and self-control.

When you pay attention to everything and everyone around you, you'll recognize beauty.

Recognize that all of your loving actions will bring you love in return.

Repay

Repay acts of kindness shown towards you with acts of kindness in return.

Repay love with more love.

Repay help offered you by helping someone else.

Repay any debt you owe or you will not be free.

Repay My love with a joyful, receptive, and grateful heart.

Rich

The word rich has been so misunderstood.

I want you to be rich.

Being rich is not just about money.

I want your life to be rich:

To have rich relationships,

Rich experiences,

To be rich in wisdom,

Rich in understanding,

And rich in knowledge.

I will fill your life with rich blessings, when you allow Me to lead you and guide you.

Rooted

I want you to be rooted in your innermost being with My Spirit.

Be rooted in love,

Rooted in peace,

Rooted in patience,

Rooted in kindness,

Rooted in generosity,

Rooted in joy,

Rooted in power and strength.

When you are rooted in Me, you will survive the wind and storms of life that would otherwise blow you off center.

Firmly rooted, you will blossom and flourish, producing fruit and standing tall.

Self-Control

One of the greatest fruits of My Spirit is self-control.

Self-control leads to patience.

Self-control leads to endurance.

Self-control leads to persistence.

Self-control leads to focus and accomplishments.

Self-control will allow you to stop negative actions that you will regret later.

When you find yourself spinning out of control, give your control over to Me.

I will help you regain your self-control so that you can be effective and fruitful.

Sense

If you love Me and follow Me, this will make sense to you.

Have a sense of kindness,

A sense of compassion,

A sense of understanding,

And above all, a sense of humor.

If you feel a sense of unrest or danger, trust those feelings and act on them.

Common sense will serve you well. Use it.

It makes no sense to Me when you judge yourself or others.

Stop judging.

I sense your every need. Trust Me.

Sense My presence. I am here with you always.

Sent

I sent you to earth to live, love, and thrive.

Therefore, you are:

Sent out to love,

Sent out to serve,

Sent out to encourage,

Sent out to forgive,

Sent out to show kindness,

Sent out to seek justice,

Sent out to show humility.

You are My eyes, ears, mouth, hands, and feet.

I've sent you to be My presence in the world.

Serve

You ou serve a grand purpose.

You serve by using your talents.

You serve through kindness.

You serve through compassion.

You serve by listening to others.

When you serve Me, above all else, I will give you strength, courage, and all that you need.

Show

When you feel lost, I will show you the way home to Me.

When doubts and fears show up, I will show you how to push them away.

When others are mean to you, I will show you kindness.

Don't be a show-off. I ask that you walk humbly with Me.

When you put your full trust in Me, I will show you the depths of My peace, love, and favor.

Slow

The world wants you to speed up.

I want you to slow down.

Be slow to anger.

Slow to judge.

Slow to worry.

Slow to react.

Slow does not mean being lazy.

Slow your pace.

I will show you the wonders of My world.

It is full of love, beauty, and peace.

Slow becomes flow when you live your life as one with Me.

Speak

I speak to you in many ways when you pay attention.

I speak through a smile given by a stranger when you open a door for them or perform an act of kindness.

I speak through the daffodil that appreciates the arrival of spring. It stretches its beautiful yellow

head toward heaven, drinking in renewed life after laying dormant, in the cold, dark ground all winter.

My language is love. I speak to you through movies and books and songs.

I speak through the giggles and laughter of your children to remind you not to be so serious.

I speak through pets who give their love unconditionally.

Pay attention to My voice.

My creation and loving presence will speak to you throughout the day.

Spirit

I have given you a mind, body, and spirit.

The spirit is the strongest of all.

When times get tough, it is your spirit which tells you to keep the faith, to have hope.

My Spirit is also within you.

It is the Spirit of Power, Love, Truth and Light.

You must care for your mind, body, and spirit and nourish each one.

The spirit thrives on stillness, beauty, inspiration, and love.

Your spirit speaks to you.

It holds truth and wisdom.

Pay attention and listen to your spirit.

Your spirit and My Spirit are in unity, so there can be no confusion or unrest, only peace and clarity.

Test

I will put you to the test to have you fully trust in Me.

When you do, you live life in a spiritual flow.

Test your relationships. Make sure they enrich you and not deplete you.

Test your heart. Let it be pure and authentic.

Contrary to what you think, you never test My patience.

I only want the best for you.

My words have stood the test of time.

When you believe them and know how much I believe in *you,* you will pass the true test to live life to the fullest.

Treasure

Be careful not to focus on amassing great treasure. This treasure requires vigilance to ward off thieves that could steal.

Instead, acquire treasure in your love and friendships.

Treat others as treasure and *you* will be a treasure.

Up

You must never give up.

You must never think your time is up.

Instead, you must feel that you are up to any challenge, because I am with you.

Don't get caught up in negative thinking.

I will build you up when you are down.

I will stir you up and wake you up to new possibilities.

I am your God of strength in times of trouble.

Give up your cares and burdens and leave them up to Me.

Your strength returns when you look up to Me.

Water

The earth is made up mostly of water.

You are made up mostly of water, too.

Water is life-giving.

My water is living water.

It satisfies the longing of your soul for love, joy, purpose, and meaning.

Seeking outside of yourself for fulfillment will cause you to constantly thirst.

Drinking the water of instant gratification, misplaced power, pride, and distraction will not satisfy your thirst long-term.

Remember your baptism.

Going under the water was letting go of the only material life you knew.

Coming up from the water symbolized a new beginning, new breath, a new life born in Spirit.

If you are thirsty, reach out for My living water.

I will renew and refresh you.

Within

When you take this time with Me, within minutes, you will feel My peace.

When the world becomes noisy and chaotic, go within and find stillness and silence.

When circumstances knock you off your feet, go within and find your center.

Your truth is within you.

My love and power is within you.

When you are overwhelmed on the outside, go within.

Chapter 5

Guidance

Life will confront you with decisions you will need to make. It's important to seek guidance, because there are things you can't possibly know.

You don't know how every decision you make will turn out or what the consequences will be as a result of your decisions.

I have given you several built-in guidance systems. They are your mind to check facts, your intuition and feelings to feel what is right or wrong, and your heart and spirit for discernment. In addition, I have given you My Spirit within you to help discern what is true.

That doesn't mean you can't seek guidance from others that you trust. Only *you* will know what feels right to you.

When you seek guidance, you will receive it. Guidance is a continuous process, because you are on a journey that started at your physical birth. Don't ever let bad decisions stop your progress. There are no wrong turns, only detours.

I am your Guide. I will guide you out of your darkness into your light. I will guide you away from lies to the truth. I will guide you away from feeling lost to finding your way.

When you seek guidance, pay attention. My direction can come in the tiniest of signs; from a butterfly landing next to you to a neon sign in front of you. Even though you walk by faith and not by sight, I love giving you guidance that you *can* see. I am the God of surprises. I love surprising you. When you ask and trust Me, I will give you guidance.

Already

I am already waiting to help you before you ask.

I already know the future and the wonderful plans I have for you.

I am already working behind the scenes to answer prayers.

You already have all that you need inside of you to become all that I created you to be.

You already have My full love, support, and approval.

When you spend time with Me each day, I will make you aware that you already have the knowledge, courage, and strength to face challenges and obstacles that will come your way.

Answer

When you call, I will answer.

I will answer in any number of ways; with signs in the form of nature, words spoken to you, books, songs, or people I will bring into your life.

I will answer through intuition.

I will answer through healing.

I will answer by causing you to feel a sense of peace or a disturbance in your spirit.

Answer to no one but Me.

Not because I am harsh or judging.

No! It's because I love you and know what is best for you.

It's because I answer in truth.

But you must do your part – be patient, listen, and pay attention.

Expect Me to answer.

Any

When you have any confusion, come to Me. I will make things clear.

When you feel any fear, call on Me, I am here.

When you have any worries turn them over to Me.

Anytime,

Anyplace,

Any challenge that you face,

I am here to answer and fulfill any need.

Anyone

Don't let anyone steal your joy.

Don't let anyone steal your peace.

Don't tell just anyone the true desires of your heart.

Anyone can hurt you, so you must be discerning when it comes to their motives and actions.

Don't let anyone tell you that you can't do something.

Anyone can talk.

Few will follow through.

If anyone can do it, that anyone is YOU.

Ask

I t brings Me great joy when My children ask for things.

Asking involves awareness.

Asking is a two-way street.

Ask and I will answer, but you must pay attention. The answer may not be what you were expecting, but the outcome will be infinitely greater.

The answer may be subtle, through a feeling of peace, an action through another person, or a deadline that may come and go.

Sometimes you must wait after you ask. But remember, I am the keeper of endless opportunities and hold endless answers.

Without having to ask, I gave you My Son who showed you the way to live and to overcome the challenges on your earthly journey.

I gave you My Spirit to lead you and guide you to help you live with infinite possibilities and potential.

Ask for anything with a pure heart and I will answer with a pure heart.

Ask and believe.

Ask and receive.

Bear

When life gets too overwhelming to bear, come to Me. I will bear your burdens.

Never forget, as My child, you bear a resemblance to Me.

That means you bear traits of kindness, gentleness, patience, generosity, love, and peacefulness.

I will never give you trials and tribulations more than you can bear.

In tough times you will bear faith and courage.

You may bear off course.

That's when you need to bear down and focus on My guidance to get you back on track.

Bear in mind that I am always with you and will never leave you.

Before

Wherever you go, I go before you.

Before you even ask, I know what is on your heart.

Before you start rushing into another day, take a moment to be still and breathe in My presence.

Before you start to complain, stop and count your blessings.

Before you drift off to sleep, think about your day. Give thanks for all that you have.

If you have challenges, turn those over to Me.

Never forget that I am with you always.

I will always love you.

I even loved you before you were born.

Between

There is only one choice you need to make each day.

You must choose between fear and love.

The outcome means choosing between light and darkness,

Between peace and anxiety,

Between hope and despair,

Between forgiveness and resentment,

Between joy and suffering.

The difference between choosing love and fear means choosing either freedom or bondage.

My grace, mercy, and love have set you free.

Nothing can stand between us.

Choosing love makes the difference between feeling triumphant or defeated.

Choose love.

Can

You can come to Me at any time. I am always here.

You can express your joy.

You can express your sorrow.

You can express your anger (I can take it).

You can turn your concerns over to Me, so I can lighten your mind, heart, and spirit.

You can see My presence in nature, in acts of kindness, and on others' faces.

When you need help that is beyond your own strength, I can send others to help you.

You can do anything when it is true and worthy.

Of this, I can assure you.

Careful

Be careful and listen to what I have to say.

Be careful what you feed your mind.

Be careful what you feed your body.

Be careful of your thoughts.

Fear, shame, and judgments will wear you down.

While I don't want you to be careless, I also don't want you to be so careful that you don't take risks.

Risking and trusting in Me will help you to grow.

Do not fear! I keep careful watch over you.

Decide

You can easily become frustrated and stuck because you fail to decide what it is that you want.

I am waiting to give you guidance and resources to help you when you decide.

When you take responsibility for your decisions, you can correct them if they were poor, or multiply them if they were good.

When you let others decide for you, it may seem easier, but you are giving away your power.

You will have regrets if you don't decide for yourself.

Whatever challenge you face, decide.

I stand at the ready to help you, empower you, and to see your decisions through.

Do

Such a little word with such powerful consequences.

Each day you are faced with this word do:

To-do lists are a mile long.

Do you really need to do all that you think you need to do?

'Do this, don't do that,' you hear in your head.

Don't be so wrapped up in *doing* that you miss out on *being*.

On the other hand, here is what you *can do* that pleases Me *and* is life-giving for you:

Study My Word, meditate, and spend time with Me. Those are activities that, when you do them, you will become more like Me.

Don't just hear what My Word says, do what it says.

Take action in the world, or you will miss out on blessing others and being blessed in return.

Choose what you do carefully.

Easy

My yoke is easy and My burden is light.

When I ask you to take on My yoke, it is a reminder to you that we are connected.

Easy does it when your path becomes rocky.

Take it easy and stay in step with Me.

It's easy to make the right decisions when you know I am guiding you.

When you are aware that I walk beside you, obstacles will no longer block your path.

I want to show you that the path can be easy when you walk with Me, side by side.

Encounter

You never know when you will encounter guidance.

That's why you must always pay attention.

Listen when someone speaks to you. You may encounter a message that I have for you in their words.

When you encounter a fork in the road, pay attention to your instincts. They will tell you the direction to take.

When you encounter difficulty, ask for My help. I will give you strength to see you through.

When you encounter a stranger in need, help them.

In that encounter, you will see a glimpse of My face.

Encourage

Hear My loving voice whisper in your ear.

I encourage you to not give up.

I encourage you to take that next step.

I encourage you to trust Me.

I encourage you to know that you can do it.

I encourage you to break through your fear.

Trust, because I am here.

Encourage others, your children, your family, your friends.

Encourage them to fulfill their dreams.

I encourage you to fulfill your dreams too.

Expect

Expect good things to happen.

Expect Me to answer you.

Expect failure if you fail to take action or take the wrong action.

Expect forgiveness if you fail.

Expect success when you do take action and learn from failure.

Expect Me to help you.

When you surrender your doubts and fears to Me, expect the unexpected.

I expect great things from you!

Found

I am the Good Shepherd. That doesn't mean I am trying to corral you or keep you from freedom like a sheep in a single pasture. No!

But sheep can be fickle. One takes off and the others follow.

They are easily distracted. Sometimes this wandering off can lead to becoming lost.

Feeling lost and alone is a terrible feeling.

To be found again, all you need is to call on Me. I will find you. You are My sheep and My sheep know My voice.

As the Good Shepherd I will protect you and guide you. You may feel lost from time to time, but you are never lost. You are found. You are home.

I am with you always.

Future

Your future is bright ...

Your future on earth and your future in heaven.

What choices you make today will determine your future.

Make good choices.

Don't live in the future, live in the present moment.

Leave your future plans in My hands, and I will see them through.

Gate

Which gate will you enter, the wide gate or the narrow gate?

The wide gate is the easy way.

It is filled with unconscious people who neglect their health, serve only themselves, and care not for others.

It leads to the path of destruction. Avoid this gate.

The narrow gate is the blessed way and leads to the road less traveled, a path that is shared by those who are generous and kind.

Walking through the narrow gate is not always easy, but it is the gate that leads to a life of peace, joy, and fulfillment. Enter this gate.

How will you find the narrow gate?

Do what is right rather than what is easy, and I will lead you there.

Go

Before you go running out, go out knowing:

I go before you.

I go above you.

I go behind you.

I go below you, supporting you.

I go within your mind, heart, and spirit, into the secret places where fear and anxiety grow.

I help those thoughts go away.

As you go about your day, I go with you.

As you go to sleep, I am with you.

Where you go, I go.

Guide

The road may be unclear in front of you, but I will guide you so you won't get lost.

I will guide you out of your darkness into the light.

I will guide you away from danger to safety.

I will guide you on a path of peace.

Allow Me to guide your decisions, guide your heart, guide your feet in the direction that you are supposed to go.

My Spirit will guide you with wisdom and truth.

Follow My lead and I will guide you to your destiny.

Help

I yearn for My children to ask for help.

My help is available to you any time of the day or night. I am the Keeper of the universe. I never sleep.

I am here to help you. I am with you always.

Most cry to Me in times of trouble. But I am able to help at *all* times.

Need inspiration? I'm here to help provide it.

Need clarity on a decision? I'm here to help.

Need to feel peace because you're feeling anxious? I can help you find peace.

When you think of help – think:

H: I am here

E: I will empower you

L: I will listen

P: I will provide for you

Let Me help you.

Here

When you spend time here in My presence, you are fully present.

You're not thinking about the past or worrying about the future.

Here you will find peace.

Here you will find clarity.

Here you can open up your heart, mind, and imagination.

Here you will receive renewed strength and inspiration.

Not focusing *here* makes you think about getting *there*.

You will miss the peace and blessings I have here for you.

Focus on the *here* and *now* and I will get you *there*.

Hidden

Your anxiousness is never hidden from Me.

Your sadness is never hidden from Me.

Your struggles are never hidden from Me.

I am with you always. I may seem hidden because you can't see Me.

But I know and feel all your sorrow and gladness.

I stand at the ready to help you and comfort you.

My love, peace, and guidance are buried within you like hidden treasure.

Unlock the hidden places to My light.

Unlock the hidden treasure of My goodness and power within you.

How

When you come to me with needs and concerns you may use three words: please, help, or why.

You may ask for something preceded by the word please. In times of desperation help may be your only prayer. Or you may ask why did this happen?

If you truly trust Me, you will lay your burdens and requests before Me and let them go. But silently, the word how spins in your brain:

How will this be resolved?

How will I make ends meet?

How will I or a loved one get well?

How will I find employment?

How is not up to you.

How is up to Me.

If

You sometimes ask the wrong questions. These questioning doubts and fears keep you stuck. It's all because of one tiny word: If.

You ask:

What if I made the wrong decision?

What if this happens?

What if I made a mistake?

What if they say no?

What if I fail?

Questions like these keep you focused on the unknown future and stuck in feelings of anxiousness. If you use if in a different way, you will receive empowering answers.

Say, "If I listen to my heart and trust God, I know I will make the right decision.

If the worst possible outcome happens, I know I'll be okay.

If I make a mistake, I know God has something better in store for me.

If they say no, there are others who will say yes.

If I fail, I'll learn."

Understand that I am the God of second chances, no – a million chances ... *if* you trust in Me.

Insist

I insist that you drive away fear.

I insist that you drive away doubt.

I insist that you let go of worry.

I insist that you lessen your pace when your life is moving too fast.

I insist that you stop and give thanks for all that you have.

I insist that you comprehend the great love I have for you and for the world.

I insist that you share this love with all that you know through a smile, kind gesture, loving

words, or a helping hand.

Instead

Instead of rushing off to start your day, sit with Me for just a moment.

Feel My presence wanting to instantly fill you with love and peace instead of frenzy, fear, and stress.

Drink in this peace like your morning tea or coffee.

As you go about your day, truly listen to others instead of thinking what you will say next.

Pay attention to the clouds in the sky (or lack of clouds). Listen to the sounds of birds, or traffic, or a child's giggle instead of unconsciously rushing from one place to the other.

You can choose joy and not stress when you are mindful instead.

Into

As you go into this day, know that I go with you.

Into your heart I have made My home.

When you allow My presence to enter into your mind,

I will clear your anxious thoughts, and replace them with My peace.

When you allow Me to enter into your dark, hidden places,

I shine My light to wipe out your darkness.

Trust in Me and I will turn your:

Fear into courage,

Failure into glory,

Stress into peace, and weakness into confidence.

Journey

You are on an eternal, spiritual journey.

The road you have chosen is a road less traveled. Most people journey on a crowded

highway moving at great speed.

Their journey is filled with tight deadlines and no time for site seeing, unaware of the landscape flying by.

The spiritual journey is taken with eyes wide open, fully aware, acknowledging every entrance, straightaway, turn, exit, and detour.

The landscape on the spiritual journey is punctuated with beautiful, scenic panoramas.

Beautiful souls encountered on the spiritual journey become traveling companions.

Have a vision for your journey.

Trust Me as your Guide.

Enjoy the journey you have chosen with Me at you side.

Lead

I want you to lead a full life.

So, follow My lead.

I will lead you over, around, or through life's challenges.

I will lead you through suffering into joy.

I will lead you out of your darkness into light.

I will lead you out of despair into hope.

Take My lead and help others as I have helped you.

Then you will not lead a life of regrets.

You will lead a life full of love, peace, fulfillment, and contentment.

Leader

Y ou are a leader whether you think so or not.

If you are a parent, you are a leader.

If you are a brother, sister, aunt, or uncle, you are a leader.

As My child you are a leader.

You are to be a leader in love,

A leader in compassion,

A leader by example in humility, justice, and kindness.

I am your Leader. Follow My lead.

Light

I am Light. In Me is no darkness at all.

My light of truth and love will shine in your dark places.

When exposed, healing can happen, shedding light to scatter the darkness.

I will light your way.

I will make your load light when you cast your cares on Me.

I will shed light on decisions you need to make, so that you have peace, clarity, and a sense of direction.

See the light.

Embrace My light.

Be a light to others.

Live

I want you to live your life knowing that you are fully loved and accepted by Me.

That means you can live a life of peace.

You can live in harmony with one another.

My Spirit resides within you.

Live by faith and not by sight.

Do not live in fear.

Live and love.

Live with My power within you.

Live each day with thanksgiving.

I want you to live up to My expectations so that you can live out your destiny.

Live your life to the fullest, shining brightly, My precious child of light.

Longing

If you are longing for direction, I will guide you.

If you are longing for peace, I will provide it.

If you are longing for strength, I will sustain you.

If you are longing for purpose, I will help you find it.

If you are longing for wholeness, I will help you put the broken pieces back together.

If you are longing for love, I will fill you with love that overflows.

I long to fulfill all of your longings.

Narrow

Narrow is the path that you have chosen with Me.

It is intimate because it is not wide but narrow.

Sometimes the path is easy and sometimes it's very difficult.

But that is true on life's journey.

Many wide roads lead to destruction.

That means it's easy to be swept along with the crowd.

There are many distractions that can take you in directions that can harm you.

Don't be narrow in your thinking.

Judging yourself or others through narrow-minded thoughts can cause great harm.

Trust Me. I will protect you, nourish you, guide you, and keep you on the straight and narrow.

Near

Stand near fire and it will warm you. Stand too near and you will get burned.

Get too near to those who gossip or tear others down and you will find trouble.

Stay near to those with high integrity who will love and support you.

Support those who are near and dear to you.

When setbacks and tribulations seem to dash your hopes and dreams, don't give up!

Victory is near!

Draw near to Me and I will see you through.

Need

I f you are in need of help, I am here.

If you are in need of comfort, I am here.

If you are in need of love, I am here.

If you are in need of peace, I am here.

If you are in need of direction, I am here.

I will take care of all of your needs.

You need not worry when you call on Me.

New

When you chase new experiences, new jobs, new relationships for the sake of thrill and excitement, eventually you will not be able to keep up such an exhausting pace.

I want to create in you:

A new mind,

A new heart,

A new spirit,

And a new zest for living.

With Me, life will be thrilling and exciting in a brand-new way.

That's because I make everything new.

Next

When you constantly think about what's next, you miss the joy in the present moment.

You seek the next move, the next opportunity, the next relationship.

The fact is that you don't know what will happen:

The next day,

The next year,

The next five years,

The next ten years,

Or even the next moment.

Only I do.

The next time you find yourself questioning what is next, stop and focus right now in the present moment.

I will guide your next steps.

Offer

You have much to offer the world.

Offer your love.

Offer kindness.

Offer compassion.

Offer wisdom.

Offer encouragement.

Offer your gifts and talents.

The more you offer the world, the more you will receive in return.

I offer you My unending love, guidance, and peace.

Path

The spiritual path is a road less traveled.

On a positive note, you will not have to fight traffic! It is not crowded.

But, due to so few traveling companions, you may feel lost from time to time.

That's when you need to trust in Me as your Guide. You are never alone. You are never lost.

While others have created a path that you wish to follow, you must forge a path of your own.

Take My hand and I will help you forge a path with purpose, meaning, joy, peace, and contentment.

Patience

You live in a world obsessed with speed and instant gratification.

Anything worthy takes time and patience. A mother does not and cannot hurry the process of birth. It takes nine months of patience for her child to be fully ready to be born. She patiently waits, but actively takes care of her baby.

I am birthing ideas and guidance within you when you patiently listen and wait for the outcome to unfold.

When you have patience, you eliminate the need for anxiety. That's because patience means resting in Me.

Just like a new mother to be, draw upon the power of patience. The peaceful, purposeful wait will be worth it.

Pattern

L ife with Me creates a beautiful pattern of color and vibrancy.

My Son set the pattern for you to follow. This pattern is woven together with threads of:

Love,

Compassion,

Peace,

Joy,

Service,

Contentment,

Power.

Don't follow the pattern of the world. It will cause you to tangle up in knots of fear or unworthiness.

Follow My pattern and your life will become a masterpiece.

Prepare

Prepare to receive blessings from Me today.

Prepare your mind by being open to new thoughts or ideas.

Prepare your speech by thinking before you react in a thoughtless manner.

Prepare your heart and spirit by being open and receptive to new opportunities and people that I send your way.

I prepare the way before you when you trust Me to be your Guide.

Provide

I provide for all of your needs.

When the storms of life descend upon you, I provide shelter.

When you get into trouble or reach a dead-end, I provide a way out.

When your heart is anxious, I will provide peace.

When you are not sure which way to go, I will provide direction.

Don't worry. I provide for the flowers and the birds.

Imagine how much more I provide for *you* My precious one.

Quick

In your world you want everything to be quick.

I want you to be:

Quick to love,

Quick to forgive,

Quick to help,

Quick to trust,

Quick to listen,

Quick to understand,

Quick to leave unhealthy relationships.

You can cut people to the quick when you react with harsh words spoken too quickly.

Think before you speak.

Be quick with your requests for help from Me.

I will be quick to putting the answers into motion.

Ready

I am ready to guide you.

Ready to empower you.

Ready to bless you.

Ready to bestow abundance upon you.

Ready to help you.

Ready to calm you.

Ready to comfort you.

I stand at the ready.

Are you ready to receive?

Require

I require that you seek justice.

I require that you love kindness.

I require that you be truthful.

I require that you clear your mind of fear, worry, and doubt.

If that is difficult, I require that you seek My help.

I require your trust, otherwise I cannot help you.

Lastly, I require that you walk humbly with Me in order to truly thrive.

Respond

I will respond when you call.

I will respond immediately with peace.

I may not respond immediately with an answer.

Some requests are complicated and take time for Me to respond.

This time may be waiting on a response from others.

I may respond in a way you weren't expecting.

You can interpret this as good or bad.

Know that I only want the best for you.

Take time when you respond to others. Don't be tempted to react in haste.

Respond to My voice. I love to know that you hear Me.

Return

You will turn away from Me at times.

I know it's hard. You can't see Me.

You get busy.

You're striving, achieving, or just getting by to provide for yourself or your family.

Maybe you've messed up and are hiding from Me.

The truth is, I am always here with open arms to provide all that you need.

Return to Me when you feel lost.

Return to Me when you are weary. I will give you rest.

Return to Me. I am not here to judge you but to love you in return.

Right

I've given you the right to do what you want.

But, I want you to do what is right.

Don't always make it a point to be right.

You will alienate others.

If it seems I don't answer right away, it may not be the right time for the answer.

Know I am working behind the scenes.

Ask me for guidance and I will point you in the right direction.

When you need to make a decision, listen to your heart.

You will know what is right.

Never fear. I am with you right now and for always.

Search

Search for answers and I will give them.

Search for peace and I will grant it.

Search your heart for truth and treasure.

If you search for something blindly or not with good intentions, give up your search.

I search the world for those open to My call.

Come to Me if you search for love, peace, and direction.

For these things, you need not search anymore.

Seek

Do not stress My little one.

Do not allow your seeking to miss the joy in finding.

I said, "Seek and you will find."

Seek peace and you will find it.

Seek love and you will find it.

Seek understanding and you will find it.

Seek direction and you will find it.

Seek clarity and you will find it.

When you find what you seek, put it into practice.

Relax, rest, enjoy, and apply what you find.

To seek is an ongoing process.

Don't allow seeking to turn into restlessness.

Let me whisper these words to you: Seek|Find|Grow.

Side

I am always at your side,

On your side,

By your side.

You have nothing to fear when you realize that when you venture forth each day, **we** venture forth together, side by side.

Stand

Stand with Me and together we can help transform the world.

Stand up for someone if they are being mistreated.

Stand out by being kind and compassionate when others are rude and uncaring.

Stand for values like honesty, integrity, and justice.

Trust in Me and I will let nothing stand in your way.

I stand always at the ready to lead you, guide you, help you, and love you.

Take

Today I am not asking you to give. I am asking you to take.

Take My hand. I will never let you go.

Take My lead, you will never get lost.

Take My love. Let it pour over and through you filling you with joy and peace.

Take the gifts of My Spirit: kindness, patience, generosity, faithfulness, gentleness, and self-control.

Take My courage.

Take My strength.

Take My power.

Take heart! I am with you wherever you go.

Teacher

A teacher can have a significant influence on you. This influence can build you up or tear you down. Teachers come in many forms.

A parent is a teacher.

A pastor is a teacher.

The obvious is a school teacher.

Life is a teacher.

The greatest teacher of all is your inner teacher.

This teacher is your soul.

It speaks the truth.

When you allow all the outside teachers to answer questions and to guide you, you may become lost.

I gave you this inner teacher.

This teacher knows the answers to your questions.

Listen to your inner teacher. It dances with My Spirit to guide you to your destiny with peace and certainty.

There

Where there is love, there can be no fear.

Where there is light, there can be no darkness.

Where there is joy, there can be no sadness.

Where there is peace, there can be no confusion.

The future is out there. The present is here.

Only I know what the future holds.

Stop trying to get there and trust Me in each moment.

There are wonderful blessings *now* and great things I have in store for you to come.

This

Rejoice! This is the day that I have made.

This day, take Me with you.

This day, slow down, don't rush.

This day, savor each moment.

This day, do something you've been putting off.

This day smile at strangers.

This day, say, "I'm grateful for," if you catch yourself complaining.

Each day is a gift.

Take this gift of a new day and use it to the fullest.

Toward

Look toward Me.

Flowers look toward Me each day. They rise up in beauty. I provide for their needs with sunshine and rain.

When you look toward Me, I will supply your every need.

Move toward your dreams.

There is no need to worry, stress, struggle, or strive.

Look toward a bright future.

Look toward your Creator, your Source of perfect Love and all that you need.

Look toward Me.

Traveler

You are a traveler on an earthly journey taking a spiritual path.

Receiving My Spirit within you provides a built-in compass to direct your steps.

The path is eternal.

Such a long journey requires provisions.

It also means traveling light.

If you haven't already, drop the weight of the past: mistakes, wrong doings, judgments, hurts. They will weigh you down and you won't get very far.

Take with you: faith, hope, love, perseverance, peace, forgiveness, patience, kindness, generosity, gentleness, and self-control.

Remember, I am not only your traveling Companion, but I am your Guide.

Unless

Unless you put your trust in Me, you will continue to experience fear and doubt.

Unless you trust Me to guide you, you will continue to wander and lose your way.

Unless you trust your own still small voice within you, you will continue to be influenced by the outside voices that may not have your best interests at heart.

Unless you speak up and speak the truth, no one will hear you. Only I can read minds.

Unless you forgive, your spirit cannot be free.

Unless you speak clearly and from a place of love, you may not be understood.

Unless you allow Me to love you, you won't experience the abundant life I want to give you.

Wait

Frustration happens easily when you have to wait. You live in a material world where you must wait.

You wait in a doctor's office.

You wait at a red light.

You wait to talk to an operator on the phone.

You wait for test results.

Don't allow anxiety and stress to fill moments when you must wait. Use this time to connect with Me.

When you ask Me for help with a sincere and grateful heart on big plans and dreams that you have, I may ask you to wait.

I am working behind the scenes on your behalf. A worthwhile request takes time.

Wait, but don't be idle.

I will renew your strength.

As *you* wait, *I* can't wait to show you what great things I have in store for you as you trust in Me.

Way

You will find a way out of your troubles when you trust in Me.

When you get out of your own way, you allow Me to open up the way to receive peace and blessings.

Give way to anxiety and fear and you will lose your way.

When you don't know which way to turn, be still.

I will show you the way.

When you wander off and get lost, find your way back to Me and I will guide your steps.

The more you make trusting Me a way of life, the richer and more joyful your life will be.

With

I am with you always.

I fill you with courage when you feel afraid.

I fill you with peace when you feel anxious.

With My nudging, I help you make decisions and direct your steps.

With tender love, I look upon you.

With Me all things are possible.

Willing

I seek hearts that are willing.

Are you willing to risk?

Are you willing to love?

Are you willing to take that first step?

Are you willing to try?

I am always ready and willing to guide you and help you when you are willing to trust in Me.

Yes

I want you to say yes more often.

Say yes when your body tells you that you need rest.

Yes, the world will go on without you.

Yes, that's right, you don't need to carry the world on your shoulders.

But, absolutely yes, the world *needs you*. It needs your best and brightest self to show up.

Say yes to an instinct or idea and act. If you don't, the opportunity may be lost.

Say yes to doing something that may scare you but will be good for you.

That's saying yes to growth and courage.

Say yes to something silly. It will lighten your spirit.

When you do these things, I say, "Yes!"

Saying yes means trusting Me.

When you trust in Me, you can do anything.

Yet

I tell you not to worry, yet, you worry.

I tell you that I will keep you in perfect peace when your mind is focused on Me. Yet, your mind drifts away.

I tell you how much I love you. Yet, you dismiss that love by feeling unworthy.

You get impatient when your prayers aren't answered quickly enough.

I'm saying, "Not yet. There is work to do behind the scenes."

I tell you, "Fear not." Yet, you're still afraid.

Yet, here you are, yet again, seeking My help and guidance.

That means you haven't given up yet.

Always remember that eye has not seen, nor ear heard, nor human heart conceived, what I've yet prepared for you.

The best is yet to come.

Chapter 6

Healing

To live life with freedom and lightness, you must heal all of your wounds. I created you to be happy and whole. When you feel life weighing heavily upon you, I want you to cast your cares upon Me, so that I can lighten your mind, body, and spirit.

Life has wounded many of My children. Wounds cannot fully heal until they are brought to light. You can cover up the pain of wounds with busyness, distractions, and numbing. But wounds will not completely heal until they are cleaned out and properly dressed.

Some wounds will take longer to heal than others: betrayal, mistrust, abandonment, rejection, shame, unworthiness, regret – these are all deep wounds that require healing.

If these wounds are not healed, you will carry pain with you consciously or unconsciously. This pain is heavy. These wounds open you up to disease and dis-ease.

Show Me your wounds. Allow Me to heal you and restore you to health and wholeness. I want to heal your broken heart, body, and spirit, but under one condition: you must want to heal.

Accept

Accept My love and grace.

It is My gift to you.

Accept the fact that you cannot change the past.

You can learn from it though.

Accept the hurts caused by others. Forgive them in your own heart and let your hurts go.

Accept responsibility for your actions.

Seeking guidance will help you make good choices when you listen and accept it.

Accept others for who they are. They are My children just like you.

Accept the seasons of life from youth to old age.

Fighting these stages causes you suffering when you could be harvesting wisdom.

When you fully accept how much I love you and want only the best for you, nothing can stop you.

Allow

Society has taught you to be self-sufficient. Rarely do you ask for help, even when you need it.

When you ask for help, you try to control outcomes.

You get in your own way.

I am here to help you, but you must allow Me to do that.

Allow Me to love you with My perfect love.

Allow Me to provide for your every need.

Allow Me to heal the hurts and suffering inside of you.

Allow Me to lead you and guide you.

Allow Me to help you so that you can live your life with ease.

Armor

Armor is necessary in battle for protection.

And in life, the slings and arrows launched by friends, family, and others cause you to put on armor of a different kind.

Sometimes, you become so hurt, you never take off your armor.

To gain My protection and love, you must relinquish your armor.

Unguarded, and open-hearted, I shall protect you.

I shall be your Armor.

Because

I am not the God of because I said so.

I created you and gave you a will of your own because I love you.

You don't believe that you are My beloved, because you listen to other voices, including your own, that tell you that you are not enough.

I sent My Son because I wanted to show you what was possible when you live your life with Me leading and guiding you.

I created the universe for you.

I sent My Word to you to encourage you.

I sent My Spirit to dwell within you to comfort and guide you.

I did all this, because I love you.

Begin

Begin your day with Me. I will fill your thoughts with peace and promise.

Life's demands can drive you into a state of overwhelm where you won't know where to begin.

Thoughts of fear or unworthiness can keep you from moving forward towards your dreams. You can easily become stuck.

Whatever you seek, begin.

Begin to trust Me.

Begin to trust others to help you.

Begin to trust yourself.

Don't worry about the outcome.

Begin again and again and your life will be filled with peace, purpose, and contentment.

Believe

My children believe in Me but, sadly, don't believe in themselves.

Believe you are loved.

Believe you are whole.

Believe you are worthy.

Believe you are able.

Believe it's your time.

Believe I am yours.

Believe you are Mine.

I believe in YOU.

Care

Care for yourself.

If you don't, you can't effectively care for others.

Care what you say.

Care how you spend your time.

When you put your trust in Me, you won't have a care in the world.

I am the supreme Care Giver.

I care for you.

Carry

I know that at times you find it hard to carry on.

Don't carry your burdens; turn them over to Me.

Don't carry around worries about the past, or future.

This will carry you away from the present moment where you live life to the fullest.

Silence these worries. I will carry you through.

Your words carry a lot of weight. Be careful how you use them.

That means being conscious of your self-talk and conversations you carry on with others.

Always speak with love and kindness.

Carry My presence in your heart.

I will carry out all the wonderful plans I have for you when you trust in Me.

Dance

Stop your running.

Drop your worries and cares.

Dance with Me.

Dance to the harmony of our spirits as one.

Let your heart dance with love and lightness.

Allow your mind to dance in wide open spaces of beauty and wonder.

Dance to a new rhythm of life in perfect harmony with Me.

End

End your striving.

End your straining.

End your troubled thoughts.

If you are constantly making ends meet, stop!

I am the God of abundance.

I'll put an end to your worries.

Begin and end your day knowing that My love for you has no end.

Expose

When you expose your inner-most pain to me, I will heal your wounded places.

When you expose shame, guilt and regret, it has nowhere to hide. It can no longer fester and grow.

When you feel engulfed in darkness, I will expose you to the light. It is the light of freedom, love, and promise of a bright present and future with Me.

Get out of your comfort zone.

Expose yourself to different people and cultures.

Expose yourself to new places and scenery.

When you do, you will expose joy and greatness hiding within you.

Fail

To fail is part of living.

Fail quickly so that you can learn and then quickly succeed.

You fail many times because you fail to fully trust Me.

You may be afraid to trust because others have let you down.

You may fail to trust because you don't believe enough to trust in yourself.

Never fail to understand My love and devotion to you.

I have great confidence in you. With Me all things are possible.

Trust Me, lean on Me. I am here to help you succeed in anything without fail.

Fear

Fear is an instinct that I gave to you. Fear is essential to help you avoid danger.

But, fear, if nurtured, like anything that you give attention to will grow. Like a garden overcome with weeds, fear can fill your mind, heart, and spirit choking the life out of you.

Sadly, My children fear Me and run *away* from Me instead of running *to* Me.

That's why, when I sent My angel messengers, they always announced their presence with these words: fear not.

I gave you an instinct *for* fear, but not a spirit *of* fear.

I love you with a divine, unconditional love. It is perfect. Where there is perfect love, there can be no fear.

So, fear not.

Glad

This is a new day that I have made! Rejoice and be glad!

A glad heart is a grateful heart.

Your spirit becomes glad when you surrender your worries and cares to Me.

Your light will shine and make others glad when you allow My peace, love, and kindness to shine through you.

You make Me glad when you rest and trust in Me.

Heal

To live a life of freedom you must heal all of your wounds. Wounds cannot fully heal until they are brought to light. You can cover up pain with distractions and numbing.

The wounds will not heal until they are cleaned out and properly dressed.

Is your wound a broken heart?

I will heal it.

Is your wound abandonment?

I will heal it with My loving presence.

I will never, never leave you.

Is your wound shame or regret?

Let it go.

Whatever your wound, I will heal you and restore you to wholeness.

But you must want to heal.

Hope

If you feel that you are being swallowed up in darkness, look to Me and I will provide you with the lifeline of hope.

You will always endure the dark times. As a result, your endurance will produce character, and character produces hope. Hope never disappoints.

Hope promises that events will turn out for the best.

Having hope is to trust in Me. My hope allows you to look forward with confidence.

Seize this lifeline of My hope and hold on tight.

My hope is sure and steadfast, an unmovable anchor. I will never let you go.

Is

I love you as is.

That means you don't have to change.

Is that surprising to you?

You were created whole and with all that you needed to be happy and fulfilled.

The trouble is—you listened to family, your culture, or others to tell you otherwise.

It is time to return to the person I created you to be.

Think that is impossible?

I tell it like it is.

All things are possible with Me.

That is truly the way it is.

Joy

Make room to receive My joy.

You can only receive My joy when you don't push joy away. You push joy away by plodding along carrying the burdens that come with day-to-day life, same old, same old stress and strain.

Give those burdens to me.

Lighten up!

My joy will surprise you!

Delight you!

When you least expect it!

I am the God of joy-full surprises.

Accept My joy.

Let

Let Me tell you the secret to happiness and peace.

Let go of the past, failures, mistakes, and living in the past.

Live in the present moment.

Let yourself move forward and let Me help you.

Let up on yourself. Stop criticizing your every action.

Let down your guard. Let others in that you can trust.

Let go of your burdens and let Me carry them.

Then you can let in happiness and peace.

Life

I have given you the gift of life.

Today is a new day in your life.

Be careful not to worry.

Worry will not add to your life, but take your joy away.

Life will have sorrow.

Life will have joy.

Life will be difficult at times.

Life will also be easy at times.

When you surrender your life to Me, I will give you the strength and courage to face the difficult times.

I will also give you a life full of richness, abundance, peace, and joy.

Name

Call on My name and I will answer. I can name all of your doubts, all of your fears, all of your triumphs, all of your joys, and all of your sorrows.

Ask in My name your heart's desires. I will give them to you.

I name and claim you as My beloved.

You are so precious to Me.

Pass

When fear or anxiety confronts you, let it pass.

My peace will push it away.

If you are drowning in pain and sorrow, stop struggling. Surrender this pain to Me. I will help you pass through the pain and sorrow.

When life becomes overwhelming in any way, say, "This too will pass."

Don't pass judgment on yourself or others. If you do, an opportunity may pass you by.

What you ask for with a sincere heart I will make come to pass.

Pass the time with Me and I will fill your life with joy and purpose.

Past

My children suffer because they live in the past.

They dwell on past mistakes, past hurts, failures, and past wrongs. They can't let go of the past. In doing so, they miss out on living fully present and joyful in the present moment.

The past is behind you.

Learn from it, but leave it there.

Whatever happened is over and done. Let the past serve you and not strangle you.

The only past you need to think about is the example that My Son set in the past.

He came to show you how to live a more abundant life.

He came to embody forgiveness.

Whatever has happened in the past, My love and strength will help you get passed it.

Refresh

I want to refresh your memory, because you seem to have forgotten.

You continue to let fear have a grip on you. I have told you (constantly) to fear not.

You continue to worry. Yet, I told you not to worry. I will provide for your every need.

You still want to take control and do everything yourself. How is that working for you?

I am here to walk beside you to carry your burdens.

Be still and know that I am God.

I will refresh your weary mind, body, and soul.

Restore

I am working in your life, leading and guiding you.

Your busyness may cause you to lose sight of this.

Restore your conscious trust in Me to direct your path.

I will restore your sight to see where you have been led and where I am leading you.

I will restore your memory to recall people, events, words, or signs I have placed into your life.

When you are feeling lost or anxious, I will restore your peace.

I am your God of restoration.

Return

I long for My world to return to its original state of creation:

To return to its beauty,

To return to peace.

I long for you to return home, home to the person you were created to be, full of wonder, joy and unlimited potential.

Return your doubts, fears, insecurities, judgments, and worries to Me.

In return, I will restore your strength, joy, and confidence.

Suffer

Suffer seems an odd word that I want you to think on today.

I want you to be mindful when you suffer needlessly.

You suffer when you dwell on mistakes.

Don't chastise yourself, learn from them.

You suffer when you dwell on pain from the past.

It is past.

Feel the pain then let it go.

You suffer when you try to do everything yourself and try to make things happen.

Turn your struggles and desires over to Me.

I will make things happen.

When you suffer, I suffer.

Catch yourself when you cause your own suffering.

I don't want you to suffer.

I want you to live your life with joy and ease.

Tell

Tell Me your joys.

Tell Me your sorrows.

Tell Me your thoughts.

I can tell when you are feeling anxious even when you don't tell Me.

Tell the truth.

When you do, you will live a life of peace.

Tell if someone is being mistreated.

That is how justice is served.

Tell friends and loved ones that you love them.

Tell friends and loved ones if they are causing harm.

They may not be aware of their actions.

That doesn't mean to tell them off, but to speak from a place of love.

I tell you the truth, do not worry. Do not fear.

I will provide your every need.

I will tell you this again and again until you believe.

Truth

When you live your life from truth, you live your life in freedom.

Speak the truth.

Tell the truth.

Seek the truth.

Listen to the truth.

Speak your truth with love.

Face the truth.

Don't deny the truth when you have done something wrong or caused another hurt and pain.

Make amends quickly.

Speak the truth quickly.

I tell you the truth, living your life from authenticity and truth is the key to peace, power, and happiness.

Whole

The world will convince you that you are damaged, broken, and unworthy.

It is a lie.

I tell you the whole truth, wholeheartedly.

There is no one else like you in the whole world.

You are whole, complete, precious, My beloved.

When others criticize you, you don't know their whole story.

They lash out to feel superior. Their whole motive is to destroy.

Don't listen to them. Listen to Me.

You are worthy.

You are whole.

My love for you is greater than the whole of creation.

Chapter 7

Transformation

I know what you are thinking with a big word like transformation. You're thinking that you need to make huge changes. In a way, you're right. But in another way, you are wrong. You see, you've changed and you're not even aware that you have.

I did not give you a spirit of fear, but of power and love. In addition, I've given you the spirit of self-discipline. You are not conscious of this. You've allowed the world to change you. Wake up!

Some of you are going through the motions, oblivious to living life to the fullest with joy and meaning. Others are consumed with fear and anxiety afraid of failure or afraid of success. Still others, obsessed with success have been conditioned to seek success outside of themselves.

Some of you enjoy some freedom that prosperity has afforded you, but your lives lack meaning. When is enough, enough?

If you are to live with joy, love, and a sense of purpose, you must transform. You must change back to the person I created you to be. How would you say it? Reboot. Reset.

You may have been led to believe that you are flawed or broken. That's why you need to let go of any hurtful, judgmental words that have crippled your true essence.

Stop listening to the outside voices of the world; what you are supposed to be, do, and have. Stop listening to the critical voices in your mind. These are the voices of judgment telling you about limitations or mistakes.

My language is love, mercy, and grace. It is not the language of fear and condemnation. When you hear judgmental voices, they do not come from Me.

Stop thinking. Stop focusing on the world of form. Focus on My transforming power of love and compassion within you. My Spirit will expand your mind, heart, and possibilities. My light will shatter the darkness.

When you are conscious of My loving presence within you, you will step out of your fear, anxiety, and weakness by holding onto My strength.

The material world will no longer have a hold on you. All things will become new, when you embrace My Transforming Spirit, My Spirit of Truth. Don't ever forget that you are My child created in My image.

Aware

When you become aware, your life will transform.

Be aware of the world around you.

Be aware of what people are saying. What do they really mean?

Be aware of expressions and body language. What are people really feeling?

Be aware of other's needs.

Be aware of your own needs.

Be aware of how you say things. Are you kind?

Be aware if you are constantly reacting. Are you rushing to judgment?

Be aware of My peace, power, love, and presence within you.

When you are aware of this, you will respond to life in a positive way.

You will become aware of My love and blessings chasing you down when you truly start to pay attention.

Become

Become more like Me.

That means that instead of being anxious and fidgety, you will become calm and patient.

Instead of being quick to anger, you will become slow to react and respond appropriately.

Instead of harboring resentment, you will become someone who resolves conflicts and forgives quickly.

When you become more like Me, you are filled with love, compassion, peace, inner strength, and confidence.

My heart's desire is that you become all that I created you to be.

Best

I want the very best for you at all times.

You will come to forks in the road. You may not know the best way to go.

If you truly trust in Me, I will show you the best way. It may not seem best at the time, but it will be.

Bring the best of yourself to all that you do. Be the:

Best friend,

Best mother,

Best father,

Best sister,

Best brother,

Best son,

Best daughter,

Best worker …

Trusting in Me and being your best is the best way to live.

Celebrate

You need to celebrate more often.

Each new day is cause to celebrate.

Celebrate when you've acted out of kindness when someone was rude to you. (I see everything you know.)

Celebrate when you act from a place of love when others act out in hate.

Celebrate when you are on time instead of late.

Celebrate when you choose to forego instant gratification and make a better choice.

Celebrate when you speak up and use your voice.

Celebrate when you follow through and do what you say you are going to do.

I celebrate *all* of your victories.

I want you to celebrate too.

Child

You are My precious child.

That means you are a child of light and not of darkness.

As My child you inherit My qualities of goodness, love, power, and justice.

You are not an only child.

You have brothers and sisters all over the world.

Act like a child full of innocence, open, and full of wonder.

Don't be childish but childlike.

I smile upon you, My child.

Smile, knowing that My kingdom is your kingdom.

Comfort

I am your Safe Haven, a place where you will always find a listening ear and warm arms of comfort to surround you.

Comfort is needed in times of trouble and uncertainty, but don't allow comfort to be a place to settle into.

The mother bird carefully builds her nest to shelter her offspring from the winds and storms.

She stays with them and protects them from predators.

She feeds them and attends to their every need.

Soon the nest becomes uncomfortable. It is time to leave. It is time to let go of comfort for a moment.

But, by letting go of comfort, the bird is able to fly. It now has the entire world to experience instead of the comfort of the tiny nest.

Always be growing, but find comfort in knowing I am with you always, and, especially as you take flight.

Confidence

When you put your confidence, your full trust in Me, I pass on My confidence through you.

Fear will no longer hold a grip on you.

Through My confidence you will possess courage.

You will speak and act with boldness, because My confidence comes from a place of truth.

I put *My* full confidence in you.

All *you* need to do is put *your* full confidence in Me.

Courage

You think that having courage means facing down some great danger or accomplishing some great feat. This can be true, because great deeds take great courage.

But, it is in small actions where courage finds its home to become woven into the fabric of who you are.

Courage speaks when you speak the truth.

Courage acts when you confront someone, but confront them with kindness.

Courage waits to hear the whole story and assess a situation before acting.

Courage listens to the still small voice within instead of all the outside voices.

Let go of fear, but don't let go of My hand. I will provide courage to see you through every moment.

Delight

I delight in seeing you happy.

I delight in surprising you.

I delight in guiding you.

I delight in providing for you.

I delight in connecting you with other people who also delight in Me.

I delight in your dreams and want to help you fulfill them.

I will give you your heart's delight.

Delight in Me.

Desperate

You may think that being desperate is not a word that brings a positive image to mind. But sometimes when you are desperate, the greatest opportunities arrive.

In moments of desperation clarity and transformation occur.

That's because you seek My help in a state of raw emotion.

Desperate pleas call for My immediate deliverance. You have given up control to allow Me to truly help you and prove to you that I will deliver you.

I am desperate for My children to know that they are not alone. If you would call on Me, you would receive My love, peace, and wisdom in your time of need.

Embrace desperate times, because I am desperate to help you.

Done

Great things have been done in My name.

Horrible things have also been done in My name.

Injustice is done not because of *My* will, but because I've given free will to all.

I created you with complete mercy and grace.

My love is not contingent on anything you have done.

It is My gift to you.

If you fret because of mistakes or things you've done wrong, you turn away from Me and miss My blessings.

Be still and reflect on all of the things I have done for you.

When all is said and done, abundance, joy, and peace will be done in accordance with your faith.

When you ask and believe, consider it done.

Enlarge

Enlarge your mind by learning.

Enlarge your heart by loving.

Enlarge your imagination by just being instead of constantly doing.

Enlarge your circle of friends by being friendly.

Enlarge your level of trust by trusting, especially putting your full trust in Me.

Enlarge your vision.

I will enlarge your life with a wealth of opportunities.

Energy

Be careful how you spend your energy.

Energy can be positive or negative.

When you gossip or complain, this sends out negative energy which corrodes other souls as well as your own.

When you use your energy to worry and fret, you can become depressed and spiral downward.

When you invest your energy constantly connected to electronic devices, you deplete your spirit and block the flow of My Spirit within you.

When you use your energy to love and serve, you become energized.

Be mindful where to put your energy.

Use your energy as a source for good.

Fade

Like the vibrant colors of leaves that fade from fall into winter, your enthusiasm will fade from time to time.

Like the seasons, your enthusiasm will not fade for long.

You will feel vibrant again when you put your trust in Me.

When your strength and health begin to fade, lean on Me.

Listen to what your body needs and take good care.

Step out of the shadows.

Don't fade into the background.

My confidence is within you to step out.

Your contribution to the world matters.

Let the critical and judgmental voices fade away.

Listen to Me this day and what I have to say.

My love and power within you will never fade away.

Forgiveness

My love, grace, mercy, forgiveness, and acceptance of you is unconditional.

This forgiveness I want you to practice in your life and relationships.

You can be quick to practice forgiveness with your children, but not with other relationships.

A lack of forgiveness results in resentment, blame, and a burden that weighs you down.

Lack of forgiveness keeps you in bondage.

Sometimes the person you need to forgive the most is yourself.

Allow My forgiveness and acceptance to empower you to transform your life.

By doing so you can transform the world.

Fuel

When you are feeling empty, I will fuel you with My loving Spirit.

When you have dreams, I will fuel you with passion to carry them out.

When your passion wanes because of setbacks and/or rejections, I will fuel you with persistence and resolve.

When you lose heart, I will fuel you with hope.

When you lose faith, I will fuel you with assurance and certainty.

You are capable and powerful beyond measure.

That's because My fuel ignites and drives you to carry-out miraculous accomplishments.

Have

When you say, "I have to," whatever that something is, it causes resistance and bitterness.

You don't have to do anything.

If you decide you don't have to take your children to school, there will be consequences.

If you decide not to take medicine, there will be consequences.

Replace the words have to with choose to.

You have the power to change your attitude from bitterness to acceptance.

You choose to take your children to school to further their education.

You choose to take your medication to improve your health and well-being.

When you say, "I have had it," that is a wonderful moment!

That's when change and transformation can happen.

You have the power within you for a rewarding life.

You have access to My help and guidance 24/7 to create that rewarding life together.

Imitate

As little children, you learned by imitating.

You would imitate your father's, mother's, sister's, brother's, or friend's actions because you wanted to be like them.

Growing up as an adolescent into adulthood, you may have continued to imitate others.

Those others may have been many in the form of co-workers, bosses, or even celebrities.

You are *you*.

There is no one else like you.

It's healthy to have admiration for someone or to be inspired by them.

It's not healthy if you don't embrace your own power and uniqueness.

You are My one-of-a-kind precious child.

As your loving parent, I ***do*** want you to imitate Me.

Imitate My love, kindness, compassion, and truth.

Inward

Y ou live your life consumed with outward goals and demands.

True peace, abundance, and power result from an inward journey.

My peace, abundance, and power are within you.

I know all of your inward secrets, dreams, and desires.

When you take this time to be still with Me,

I strengthen the inward parts of you; your mind, your heart, your soul.

The inward journey equips you for the outward journey.

The deeper you travel inward, the richer your life will be.

Moment

Take a moment before you rush out to center yourself in My presence.

The moment you feel anxiety or fear, say My name. I am here at this moment.

Pay attention. At any moment I will give you a sign, bring a person to speak words of enlightenment to you, or someone to help you on your journey.

I can make circumstances change for you in a moment, in the twinkling of an eye.

The moment you surrender and trust in Me, that's the moment you will live truly free.

Neighbor

My commandment is to love your neighbor as yourself.

I am Love.

Love has transforming power.

Don't know your neighbor next-door?

Send them love.

Pray for them.

Your neighbor is more than those physically surrounding you.

Your neighbor is every man.

Your neighbor is every woman.

Your neighbor is every child.

Your neighbor is every creature that lives on the earth. Each serves a purpose, no matter how small.

Your neighbor is the forest and the mountains and the ocean.

Love your neighbor. Love.

Overcome

Grief may overcome you when you suffer a loss.

But I am with you always to comfort and to calm you.

When evil strikes, it's natural to want to strike back. But that will only give evil more power.

You must overcome evil with good.

I want you to be overcome with joy, peace, and contentment.

I created the changing sky, majestic mountains, vast oceans, cascading waterfalls, and too many plants for you to count so that you would be overcome with awe and wonder.

Remember the words of My Son who suffered trials and tribulations, even death. "Be of good cheer; I have overcome the world."

You are an overcomer too.

Perfect

You are perfect in My eyes, because I love you with a perfect love.

You live in a material world.

You measure perfection by earthly standards.

They are not My standards.

My perfect love casts out fear.

Perfect love casts out criticisms, comparisons, and judgments.

When you embrace My perfect love, you will find perfect peace.

Renew

Arise. Welcome to a new day. Call upon Me and I will:

Renew your strength,

Renew your confidence,

Renew your peace,

Renew your hope,

Renew your mind,

Renew your body,

Renew your spirit.

I am the Author of renewal and restoration when you renew your trust in Me.

Same

Almost everyone shares the same needs:

The same need for security,

The same need for acceptance,

The same need for recognition or significance.

In addition to these same needs are the same problems:

The same feelings of doubt,

The same feelings of fear,

The same feelings of unworthiness.

If you hold onto these feelings, you will become stuck.

I am the same today, yesterday, and tomorrow.

That means My feelings for you are the same.

I offer you love, security, acceptance, and significance always.

Look to Me. Trust in Me.

When you do, you will never be the same.

Seeds

My seeds of love and compassion have taken root within you.

As these seeds grow and produce fruit, the fruit will produce more seeds.

Scatter these seeds of love, seeds of kindness,

Seeds of compassion,

Seeds of hope.

Some seeds may be ignored.

Some seeds will take root for a while and die out.

However, some seeds will take root and grow deeper and deeper until fruit is produced and the cycle continues.

Love, care, and nurturing will sprout seeds of greatness.

Look to Me, your Gardener, to help these seeds grow and flourish.

Small

I don't want you to be small. I want you to be great and powerful beyond measure.

The word small is a paradox.

To be great and powerful, you must start small.

Small actions add up over time to produce greatness.

These include:

Small acts of kindness,

Small acts of courage,

Investing small amounts of time in silence and stillness soaking in My presence each day,

Small prayers of gratitude lifted up to Me,

Small actions of trust taken and surrendered to Me.

One cannot leap into greatness without taking many small action steps.

Everyone starts small.

Too many of My children stay small.

Don't stay small!

Step out and become great with My help, as you take one small step at a time.

Space

When you make space in your day to spend time with Me, I will renew your mind, body, and spirit.

Leave some space between people who crowd out your peace.

Space creates harmony.

Free up space in your surroundings.

Free up space in your mind. That means clearing out all kinds of cluttered thoughts.

When you let go of worry, concerns and suffering,
you create space to receive My expansive comfort, joy, and love.

Transform

I give you the power to transform at any time.

Transform your sorrow to joy.

Transform your fear into courage.

Transform your doubt into faith.

Transform your uncertainty into certainty.

Transform your character from apathetic to compassionate.

I am the God of transformation.

When you trust in Me, I will transform you into your full magnificence.

Want

My Son always asked those whom he met, "What do you want?"

The answer was never a material possession like a bigger home or endless wealth. The answer was in the form of healing either physical or spiritual in nature, or wanting guidance.

So, what do you want?

Most people don't step away from their busy lives to ask this question.

They simply want material possessions like the latest gadget or fashion.

Or they fill their time with jam packed social calendars wanting to be popular and please people.

I know what I want for you.

I want you to know how much I love you.

I want you to know what a unique and powerful person you are.

I want you to be wildly successful using all of your strengths and talents.

I want you to have peace.

I want you to have courage.

That list is as small as a mustard seed compared to what I want for you.

Welcome

Welcome challenges that come your way. Challenges help you to grow.

Welcome criticism when it is truthful, not mean. There can be some blind spots in your character that you may not see.

Welcome others into your life. I didn't create you to travel this life alone.

Welcome those dark parts of you to show up. Unsavory behaviors, past mistakes, hurts, shame, all need to come out of hiding.

Offer a welcome mat to them.

Visit with them. Face them. Then show them the exit. Tell them they are no longer welcome.

I welcome your pleas and petitions for help.

I welcome you with open arms to answer and provide for your every need.

Chapter 8

Truth

Y ou seek certainty, security, and comfort. This causes you anxiety and stress. What you need to seek is the truth. I tell you the truth. You will find certainty, security, and comfort in Me.

I tell you the truth. I am not judging your every action. When you allow such thoughts, you cut yourself off from Me. Without Me, you can easily lose your way. Without Me, you won't believe you have everything you need within you.

I tell you the truth. There is only one you! I love you. You are a treasure to Me. Sadly, you don't believe Me. You seek approval and direction from others who don't know what is best for you. You listen to their opinions and advice. You listen to their criticisms and judgments. They do not know the truth!

Only you can know what is true for you. I have given you instincts, feelings, intuition, natural talents, and abilities. When you pay attention to these, you know what is true.

My Spirit will guide you into truth. When you live your life in truth, you will live your life with ease. When you seek the truth, know the truth, you will know what to do.

I tell you the truth. I will never leave you nor forsake you.

My Son told you that you will know the truth and the truth will set you free. When you tell the truth, when you live from a place of truth, you let go of doubts, worry, judgments, and shame.

Speaking the truth needs to come from a place of love. True love does not cause pain. So, speak the truth and speak it quickly. Be true to yourself. Be true to others. Be true to Me. Discover for yourself how truth will set you free.

About

When difficult circumstances arise, you will pray for someone or something.

I know that you want to fix things and make things right. But, think about this. Maybe it's not about you.

Maybe I am trying to teach someone to trust in Me to provide for them.

Maybe I am drawing out some deep-seated issues they are having that have kept them stuck.

Perhaps this circumstance will allow them to break free.

Go about prayer.

Go about loving.

Go about believing.

Go about trusting in Me.

Understand though, this may not be about you.

Again

L iving and loving life to the fullest means embracing this little word – again.

Try again.

Fail again.

Forgive again.

Trust again.

Love again.

Believe again.

Hope again.

Learn again.

Start again.

I am the God of a million chances.

I will always love you and tell you I love you again and again.

Always

I am with you always.

I always want the best for you.

You can always bring Me your joys, sorrows, and concerns.

I will always listen.

I will always answer, although the answer might not always be what you were expecting.

Always trust Me.

Always seek Me.

Always have faith.

Always have hope.

I will love you and sustain you – always.

Anything

D o not be anxious for anything. Make your requests known to Me and I will grant you peace.

Anything you hold onto; grudges, guilt, shame, or blame will weigh you down and stunt your growth.

Let anything like that go, forgive yourself and others.

Come to Me with anything on your heart and mind.

Ask for anything in My name and I will give it to you.

Don't let anything keep you from knowing that I am not separate from you.

My loving powerful Spirit is within you.

That's why you can do anything with Me.

Approval

When you break your connection to Me, you lose sight of Whose you are.

Your confidence will wane. You will seek ...

Approval from family,

Approval from those you work with,

Approval from friends.

Their approval does not matter.

Only *My* approval matters.

When you seek to live your life from truth, justice, kindness, and humility, you will automatically win the approval of others operating from these same values.

You have My approval, My blessing.

You are My beloved. In you I am well pleased.

Armor

I give you My power and strength along with My armor to protect you.

This is the armor of truth, the armor of faith, and the armor of peace.

You are fighting the enemy which wants to steal your joy and peace.

The enemy attacks with thoughts of fear, doubt, and unworthiness.

Armor is meant for battle.

Armor is heavy. It is not meant to be worn all the time.

If you do, you will keep out love, intimacy, or vulnerability.

Armor's weight will cause you to grow weary.

Let your armor down so that you can truly love and live.

Use My armor when you need to fight an enemy.

My armor will protect you.

Be

Be a good listener and you will be appreciated.

Be a good friend and you will have more friends.

Be attentive and you will not only avoid danger, you will recognize opportunities.

Don't be doing all the time.

Your mind, body, and spirit will be depleted.

Be aware of My presence with you and within you.

Be still and know that I am God.

Be still and know that I AM.

Be still and know.

Be still.

Be.

Belong

Anxiety, fear, and isolation are feelings that belong to the world.

Being in the world you may find it hard to belong.

In My world you always belong.

You belong to the light.

You belong to love.

You belong to each other.

You belong to Me, but in *My* world you are set free.

Both

If you could see both sides from heaven and earth, you would see My divine plan.

You have to experience both trials and triumphs, so that the victory is much sweeter.

You must have both highs and lows or life would be one monotone note.

You will make both wise and foolish choices.

That is how you learn and grow.

You must hear both sides to every story to discern what is true.

I created both day and night for work and rest.

Rest in the fact that I love you both now and forever.

Brave

Ｙou are a brave warrior.

Your battles are not fought with swords or spears, but with truth, justice, and love.

Be brave and do not let others compromise your integrity.

To yourself and to Me you must be true.

Be brave in your relationships. Act out of love.

Be brave by forgiving yourself and others quickly.

Be brave by setting boundaries and saying no.

I want you to be brave.

Fear not!

I am with you.

I will help you be brave so that you can fight all of life's battles.

Can

You can do anything when you put your trust in Me.

You can have peace.

You can have joy.

You can be successful in your work.

You can have loving relationships.

You can overcome challenges.

You think you can do everything on your own.

That's when you can become overwhelmed.

You can, instead, let go and let me lead you and guide you.

With Me, I can help you become all that I created you to be.

On that you can be sure.

Catch

I hope you catch what I'm saying, that you are precious and whole and wonderful in My eyes.

There is no catch. I love you no matter what.

I want you to catch the same love and enthusiasm I have for you and pass that onto others.

When you create acts of kindness, you help others catch a glimpse of My kingdom.

When you start to complain or judge yourself or others,

catch yourself before a word comes out of your mouth.

You'll catch on to being more loving and compassionate.

You'll catch a spirit of gratitude instead of grumbling.

Cause

When you allow your mind to race with worry and anxiety, you cause yourself stress.

Be still.

When someone hurts you without cause, let it go.

Don't cause more trouble for yourself.

Turn the matter over to Me.

Don't cause others to stumble and fall.

Be a force for good.

When anything causes you to feel lonely, confused or lost, bring the cause to Me.

I will fill you with love, clarity, and guidance.

Find a worthy cause and give yourself to it.

Know that I am always with you, loving you and supporting you.

That will give you cause to celebrate!

Certainty

When troubles come your way, when you find yourself having to take a risk or make a huge decision, you long for certainty.

You start asking 'what if' questions. What if I make a wrong decision? What if I fail? What if this problem doesn't go away?

Be still, clear out your doubts and fears and make a decision with your heart to trust in Me.

Instead of looking forward, look back and remember the events that have brought you here right now.

Can you not say with certainty that you have come through many trials as a result of the many decisions you have made?

Certainty is like a circle. When you feel uncertain with doubts and fears, circle back and remember where I put those doubts and fears to rest.

Have certainty that I love you.

Have certainty that I am always with you.

Have certainty that all is well.

Change

You fear change, and rightfully so, especially unexpected change.

This change will upset your world.

Turn these change challenges over to Me.

The ultimate outcome may be a change for the better.

If you're sad, lonely, angry, resentful, or fearful, I will help you change your heart.

Life is like the seasons.

They change to reflect:

rest in the winter,

new life in the spring,

work in the summer, and harvest in the fall.

Change, when nurtured, means growth.

When you accept change, your life will change.

Know that My love for you will never change.

Chosen

You are chosen. You did not choose Me, but I chose you.

Being chosen does not mean excluding others.

You are chosen to find the good in others and in the world.

You are chosen to find strength in Me when the journey gets tough.

You are chosen to be a light of peace and justice in a hurting world.

If you have chosen to follow Me and trust Me, you have chosen to live an amazing life.

Come

I come to you through these words.

I come to you through each sunrise and sunset to let you know that I am in charge.

I come to you through music and song that strike a chord in you.

I come to you through others that I bring into your life.

Come to Me with your concerns.

Come to Me with ideas you come up with.

I will help them blossom and grow.

When you come through trials, give thanks for the opportunity to grow.

Hear Me whisper, "Come along with me." I will guide your way.

Remember that nothing will ever come between us.

Constant

Y ou can choose constant complaining or constant thoughts of gratitude.

When you are in constant contact with Me, your life will take on a peaceful flow.

The world is in constant change.

That's why you need to depend on me.

I am constant, always loving, always providing, never changing.

Day

Rejoice! It is a new day!

The night is over and gone.

Start your day with Me.

This day stretches out full of new promise and possibilities.

Look at this day as a day unlike any other.

This is a day to renew.

Focus on *this* day and each present moment.

At the end of the day give thanks and end your day with gratitude.

Didn't finish something you started?

Tomorrow is another day.

Deep

At times you may find yourself going off the deep end. Whether if it's real or imagined, this is the time to call on Me.

When you find yourself in deep trouble or in deep need, I am here.

My loving Spirit dwells in the deepest part of you, in the depths of your heart.

Know deep down that I am with you always.

I love you always.

My love for you runs deep.

Door

I will close a door when something is not right.

I will open a door when it is.

Close the door to your lips if you start to say something you'll regret.

Open the door to your heart to those you trust.

Close the door on failures.

Failures are over and done.

I stand at the door and knock.

Please, let Me in.

Eager

When you are eager, you can choose to be impatient or earnest.

Don't be eager to please at the expense of your integrity.

Don't be eager to make big decisions without thinking in earnest.

I am eager to help you.

I am eager to guide you.

I am eager for you to tap into My love and power within you.

Be eager to receive all that I have in store for you with patient expectation.

Endless

Time is a human concept. I have no beginning and no ending. Time is endless. So, I want you to know:

Endless are your possibilities.

Endless are the opportunities to connect with others on your life's journey.

Endless are ideas that will spring forth from you.

Endless are the wonderful plans I have for you.

Endless is My love for you.

Endure

Suffering will not endure forever.

I will not allow that which you cannot endure.

When you endure times of waiting, you develop patience.

When you endure hardships, you develop wisdom and strength.

When you endure sorrow, you can appreciate joy.

All you endure has a meaning and purpose.

When you realize that and learn from that, you will rise up in confidence and victory.

And never forget, My love for you will endure forever.

Faith

Trueue faith is based on how much trust you put in Me.

Faith shows up when the money runs out.

Faith shows up when you begin to doubt.

Faith tells you things will be alright.

Faith will get you through the night.

Faith will get you through the day.

When you feel lost, faith will help you find your way.

It is not enough just to *have* faith.

You must *act through* faith.

Faith in action is love, compassion, courage, and kindness.

I am faithful to you.

I want you to be faith *full*, and put your complete trust in Me.

Find

You can't find out the future.

You'll just have to trust in Me.

However, you'll find that what actions you take today will affect tomorrow.

Find yourself distracted and you'll waste time and get off track.

Worry and fret and you will not find peace.

Seek shelter in Me and your mind and spirit will find rest.

You don't need to seek a mountaintop experience to find Me.

You will find Me in a brief encounter, a smile, a kind gesture, a bird, a song, a word.

Seek and you will find.

Find joy.

Find love.

Find all you need in Me.

Follow

Follow along with Me ...

If you constantly follow the events in the news,

you will believe there is more evil than good in the world.

There is far more good.

Don't blindly follow friends or even people in authority.

They may not follow through on what is best for you.

Follow your heart.

Follow your dreams.

I follow you.

Follow Me.

Form

I created your form in My image. As there are three parts to Me, there are three parts to you.

Your physical form is your mind and body combined with your spiritual form which is your spirit.

Your mind will form ideas, opinions, and beliefs.

Your body will form a shape. How large or small, weak or strong depends on the care and attention you pay to your form.

Your spirit will form your true essence, your values, your true heart's desires.

Form solid habits to nurture your mind, body, and spirit.

Together, we will form a beautiful life now and for all eternity.

Freedom

You yearn for freedom, but you refuse to embrace it. Holding onto doubt, fear, and suffering keeps you from experiencing freedom.

I have given you My Spirit. In My Spirit is freedom.

You have:

Freedom to choose,

Freedom to love,

Freedom to think,

Freedom from worry,

Freedom from suffering.

Freedom comes with a price. It's letting go of the world's limitations to embrace My unlimited potential within you.

Freedom is a precious gift.

Accept this gift and express your freedom with joy.

Use your freedom for good.

Friend

You call Me your Father and I call you My child, but I am also your Friend!

A true friend supports you in good times and bad.

A true friend is there for you when you're happy or sad.

A true friend listens without giving advice.

A true friend will not judge you.

A true friend will show up when needed.

A true friend will love you, no matter what.

It is good to have friends in high places. You have the greatest Friend in Me.

Full

I want your life to be full.

Not full of busyness, not having a full calendar, or full of constant obligations. No!

I want your life to be full of meaning.

I want you to be:

Full of love,

Full of joy and laughter,

Full of compassion,

Full of understanding.

When you surrender your concerns to Me, you will know full well how wonderful life can be.

Gift

I've given you the gift of life.

You are My unique and wonderful child.

I've also given you unique talents and gifts.

Some of My children unwrap their gifts and use them to the fullest.

Some compare their gifts to others and discount them or abandon them.

Still others never open their gifts, because they are filled with feelings of unworthiness, resistance, or fear.

I am proud of you.

I love you.

You are *My* gift to the world.

Give

Give of yourself.

Give of your talents.

Give your love.

Give your encouragement.

Give your time to listen.

Give your time to help others.

Give your knowledge.

Give your heart.

Give your heart's desires to Me.

When you give, you receive. When you give generously, you receive generously.

Grace

My grace is unconditional.

You are not in My good graces one minute and in bad graces another minute.

When you comprehend how much I love you, your life will take on a sense of grace and flow.

My grace and favor will chase you down.

My grace is sufficient for you.

Believe it and claim it.

Ground

When you find yourself on shaky ground, be still and feel My presence.

I will fill you with peace and return you to solid ground.

Take care and don't push yourself so hard.

When you overdo, you can easily run yourself into the ground.

When you see injustice or when others harshly criticize you, speak up and stand your ground. My Spirit will give you the courage and the words to say.

Don't fade into the background. Step out to shine your full glory, My glory within you.

Happy

It makes Me happy when you put your trust in Me.

You become happy when you let go of worry, doubt, and fear.

It makes Me happy when you are kind, compassionate, caring, and tolerant towards others.

When you are able to fully embrace My presence, you become happy and carefree.

Joy will bubble up inside of you.

A happy heart will cause you to put on a happy face.

Like any loving parent, more than anything, I want you to be happy.

Home

I created you to find your home in Me.

My home is full of love, acceptance, encouragement, and peace.

You may not feel at home in your body with its aches and pains, anxiety, or fear.

The deepest part of you can transcend your body to find rest in Me.

Even though I have prepared a glorious home for you beyond this material world,

My home is in your heart ... always.

Honor

Honor your mother and your father, especially if they have mistreated you.

I will bestow favor and honor on you for your faithfulness.

Seek honor above all else.

Honor one another as members of My family.

Honor your mind, body, and spirit through care and nurturing.

You are My child, an heir to My kingdom.

You are clothed with My glory and honor.

Immediate

You have immediate access to Me, the Creator of the cosmos who keeps the stars and planets in their place, the Creator of you. I am with you right now and always.

You can have immediate peace. Breathe in My presence. I will hold you and rock you in My arms, taking away any anxiousness you feel.

Immediate clarity will come to you when you turn your challenges over to Me.

As long as you are aware of your connection to Me, you will receive immediate feelings of love, joy, peace, and guidance.

Intend

I intend for you to become the ultimate person I created you to be.

That means you intend to be receptive.

You intend to be loving.

You intend to be kind.

You intend to be generous.

You intend to be forgiving of yourself and others.

You intend to be compassionate.

You intend to be prosperous.

You intend to help others.

I intend to love you, support you, and fulfill all that you intend.

Involved

Be careful what you get involved in.

When you are involved with too many commitments, you will be tired and stressed.

When you are involved with too many activities at once, you divide your attention and become ineffective.

When you become involved with other people's business, be careful not to do more harm than good, for them and for you.

At the same time, be fully present and involved in your relationships, speaking love and truth.

Be fully involved in trusting Me.

It's not complicated.

All that is involved is letting go and letting Me show you what great things I have in store for you.

Know

I want you to know in your mind, heart, and spirit that what I say is true.

Know that you are My child in whom I am well pleased.

Know you are My beloved.

Know that I want the very best for you.

Know that My power and glory is within you.

Know that I am here to guide you.

Know that you can do anything with Me. All things are possible.

Be still and know that I am God, your Shelter, your Rock, your Source of life, love, joy, and peace.

Last

I am Alpha and Omega, the beginning and the end, the First and the Last.

My love for you will last forever.

Maybe, at last, you will believe how much I love you just as you are.

I want you to make a lasting impression on all that you meet.

Invest your time and resources on what will last; lasting friendships, serving others, and making a difference in the world.

The last thing on your mind should be worry or fear.

Last of all, know that I am your source of lasting love and peace.

Lavish

I love you.

You are My child.

I not only want you to know how much I love you; I want you to know the wealth of love that I have lavished upon you.

A parent will ask their child, "How much do I love you?" and the child will respond with arms open wide saying, "This much!"

Ask Me how much I love you and My arms will extend beyond the cosmos.

That's what lavish means to Me.

Lean

Lean on Me in times of trouble.

Lean not on your own understanding.

The outcome I have for you will be much greater.

Lean on Me when times are lean. Those times won't last for long.

I did not create you to be alone. Lean on others that you can trust for support.

I am your Rock.

You can trust Me.

Depend on Me.

Rely on Me.

Lean on Me.

Love

My love for you is deeper than the deepest part of the ocean.

I hope you can fathom how many fathoms that is!

No one has deeper love for you than I, because I AM LOVE.

My love for you is everlasting.

My love for you is unchanging. I don't love you one minute and not the next.

My love will support you and surround you like an embrace when you feel lost and alone.

I love you now and will love you forever.

I pour My love into you when you are willing to receive it, making My love overflow from you and out into the world.

Know My deep love for you.

Feel My love for you.

Allow Me to love you.

Then share this overflowing love with others.

More

If you find yourself lacking. If you desire more, I will give you more when you ask with a sincere heart and sincere intentions. Ask for:

More patience,

More knowledge,

More direction,

More clarity,

More kindness,

More resources,

More help,

More love,

More peace.

The more you give, the more you will receive.

The more you ask from Me, the more I will provide.

Because, no one loves you more.

Never

There will never be anyone else like you.

That's why you must never retreat to the shadows, but step into the light and claim your place in the world.

Never let anyone into your life that lacks love and understanding.

They will never seek to build you up, but to tear you down.

Never underestimate your power and My power within you.

You never have to worry when you put your trust in Me.

Fear will never have a hold on you.

Your life here is short. Never take a day for granted.

Stop stressing and striving for more. It will never be enough.

When you trust in Me, you will never be hungry or thirsty for more.

When life becomes overwhelming and troubles come, never forget My promises.

I will never leave you nor forsake you.

Never.

New

Today is a new day.

You get to make a new start.

See things with new eyes.

Appreciate all that you have with new gratitude.

The past is gone.

All things are new.

Embrace a new attitude of service.

Embrace a new day expecting new opportunities.

Each day is a new adventure with Me as your Guide.

No

Such a powerful, little word with such negative meanings. You need to say no more often to use its full power. Say no to more commitments than you can handle.

No is a compete sentence.

Then say no to guilt for saying no.

The person asking will find someone else.

Say no to worry.

It is a useless emotion.

Put your trust in Me.

Say no to the voices outside of you that say you aren't enough.

Say no to the false voice inside of you that says you aren't enough.

When you say no to doubt and no to fear, you say yes to receive My love, peace, courage, and presence within you.

Embrace the word no.

Nothing

When you trust in Me, completely trust in Me, you will lack for nothing.

Nothing can harm you.

Nothing can confuse you.

Nothing can stop you.

Above all else, nothing can separate you from My love, nothing.

One

You are one with Me.

Just as the body has many parts, these parts become one.

You are one with all of creation.

The air you breathe and the water you drink becomes a part of you; one with you.

One is a whole number. You are whole. That means you are healthy, un-broken, undamaged.

You are one person, one-of-a-kind.

My one desire for you is to feel this oneness, not once but always.

Possible

All things are possible with Me.

You have to believe all things are possible.

If possible, you must do your part to make things possible.

I said, "All things are possible *with* Me, not *for* Me."

It is more than possible that you may not get what you ask for.

Don't let that discourage you.

I am the God of all knowing.

I have much greater plans for you than you can imagine possible.

Power

My power is within you!

It's true, but you don't believe it.

Believe it!

You have the power to overcome fear.

You have the power to forgive those who hurt you.

You have the power to love those who seem unlovable.

My Spirit within you provides you with the power of peace, clarity, and vision.

Fear not! Embrace My power to live with confidence.

But don't abuse this power.

I speak the truth.

When you speak the truth, truth comes with power.

Precious

Dear one, you are a precious gift to the world.

You are precious in My sight.

Each moment that you have is precious. Become aware of that.

You are more valuable than all the rubies, diamonds, emeralds, sapphires, and every precious stone in the galaxy.

Use the precious gifts I've given you to share your value with all that you meet.

My joy overflows when you spend this precious time with Me.

Present

I am ever present.

I am present with you now.

When you dwell on events of the past, daydream or worry about the future, you miss the present moment.

The present is what creates your future.

You may not see at the present moment how all will work out. Just keep trusting Me.

Present your requests to Me.

Know that neither life, nor death, nor angels, nor things present, nor things to come, nor powers, nor height, nor depth, nor anything else in creation can separate you from Me.

Promise

I promise to never leave you.

I promise to always love you.

I promise to always keep you.

I promise to sustain you.

I promise to provide for you and provide abundantly.

I promise you freedom when you let go of your worries, doubts, and fears.

I promise that with Me all things are possible if you promise to trust and believe in Me.

Purpose

You were created with purpose and love. My children get hung up on the word purpose as if they are only meant to have one purpose.

That is not true.

The whole purpose of your life (should you choose to accept this fact) is that you find purpose every day in the many actions that you take.

My only purpose for you is that you live your life *on* purpose.

In everything live intentionally.

Your purpose is to receive and give love.

Your purpose is to become the most that you can be.

Your purpose is to use the gifts and talents I've given you.

Rejoice

I want you to rejoice!

I rejoice over you!

You are My beloved.

When you dwell on inconveniences or what you don't have, you can't rejoice.

Rejoice if you have clean drinking water at your disposal.

Much of the world doesn't.

Rejoice if you have a roof over your head and food in your belly.

Rejoice for freedom.

In Me you have freedom from worry, freedom from care.

Rejoice when troubles come your way.

They will make you stronger and wiser.

Trust in Me to see you through them.

This is the day that I have made.

Rejoice and be glad in it with Me.

Respect

To have respect, you must show respect.

Respect those in authority.

That doesn't mean you have to support them if their intentions are not true.

Respect your children.

Respect those you lead.

Respect your friends and family.

Respect the earth and all there is within.

I will respect your wishes when you come to Me with a heart that is pure.

Reward

When you stop your running and be still in My presence,

I reward you with peace.

When you stop trying to figure everything out on your own,

I reward you with wisdom.

When you get lost and give up,

I reward you with giving you direction and comfort.

When you treat others with love and compassion,

your reward is receiving love and compassion in return.

Great is your reward when you follow in My footsteps.

Risk

Risk to love.
Risk to try.
Risk to fail.

Risk to succeed.

Risk to feel.

Risk to be criticized.

Risk to be praised.

Risk to speak up and speak the truth.

Risk to let go.

There is no risk when you trust in Me.

Rock

I am your Rock and your Salvation. You need not fear.

When difficulties rock your world, I am here.

When you are in need of comfort, I will rock you in My loving arms.

When you hit rock-bottom, I will offer My hand to lift you up.

I am your Redeemer, your Refuge, your steadfast Rock.

Safe

In Me you will find a safe place.

I will not judge you.

I will not harm you.

I will only love you.

It's safe to say that I created you to love you.

Your secrets are safe with Me. Tell Me what they are so that your heart and conscience can be free.

When you feel safe, you feel peace.

When you feel fear, come to Me. I will provide a safe haven for you to rest.

Saved

It is by My grace that you are saved.

It is a gift! You don't have to do anything but accept it.

You are saved from trying to please Me. I am already pleased with you. I created you, remember?

You are saved from guilt.

I've forgiven you for all you have done. Why do you want to hold onto it?

You are saved from shame. Shame cripples. Let it go.

You are saved from an aimless life. I fill you with peace and purpose, guiding your every step.

Goodness and mercy will follow you every day of your life.

I've saved the best for last … you will be with Me forever.

Say

You say, "Help." I say, "I'm here."

You say, "Why?" I say, "There's more going on than you know. Have patience."

You say, "How?" I say, "Leave that up to Me."

You say something is unforgivable. I say, "Forgive and let it go."

You say, "I don't have strength to do this anymore." I say, "Don't give up. My strength is found in your weakness."

You say, "I'm afraid." I say, "Fear not. I am with you."

You say, "I don't know what will happen." I say, "That's right! That's why you need to trust Me that all is well."

You say, "Thanks." I say, "You are welcome. Now, you are getting somewhere."

Say thanks in all circumstances.

I have the final say. That is to know that what I say is true.

I am here for you.

I love you.

I long for you to say you love Me too.

Security

You seek security in a job, but circumstances can change in an instant.

You seek security in a home and possessions, yet you fear thieves will break in and steal.

You seek security in relationships, but if other's hearts are not true, your security is shattered.

Seek security in Me. I promise you peace, abundance, love, and true security.

Shine

You are the light of the world! Let your light shine!
I shine My light upon you.
My light of glory shines within you.

That's how *you* shine.

Shine your light of love.

Shine your light of joy.

Shine your light of truth.

You are My lamp of great light shining into a world full of darkness.

Shine brightly!

Silence

The great oak tree grows in silence.

The stars and planets hold their places in the cosmos, all in silence.

In silence, a baby begins its growth in the womb.

The world is full of noise.

My language is silence.

But, that doesn't mean I am not seen or heard.

Silence your thoughts a few moments to sit in the silence of My presence.

I will silence your worries and fears and fill you with My peace and love.

Source

I am your River of Source. We flow as one.

When you feel drained and weary, stop and let go. I am your Source for rest.

When you've been hurt, allow My Source of love to comfort and surround you.

When you feel confused, tell Me about your confusion. I am your Source for clarity.

If you are drowning in anxiety and fear, hang on tight to Me. I am your Source for relief and salvation.

I am the Source of love, peace, joy, abundance, strength, creativity, compassion, and hope!

My Source is unlimited.

When you are conscious of My Source flowing through you, there is nothing we can't do together.

Start

Every day is a new start.

Start noticing everything around you.

Start paying attention to the tone of your voice.

How do you talk to yourself?

How do you talk to others?

Start something you've wanted to do, but you've been putting off.

Start this day knowing how much you matter to Me, because I've loved you from the start.

Steadfast

My love for you is steadfast. It is a firm and unwavering love.

That means I love every part of you *all* the time.

When you stumble or make mistakes, I am there to catch you and help you to recover.

I am not turning away from you or judging you.

Unfortunately, when you make mistakes, you usually turn away from *Me*, feeling shame and condemning yourself and your actions.

I am not ashamed of you. I am not judging you. My love for you is steadfast, constant, loyal, unwavering.

Supply

When you are troubled, I will supply you with peace.

When you are lonely, I will supply you with My loving presence.

When you are hurt, I will supply you with comfort and hold you in My loving arms.

When finances are sparse, I will supply you with provisions.

When you feel defeated, I will supply you with strength and courage.

I am your Storehouse, your endless Supply.

Sure

In the material world you have much uncertainty. But My Kingdom is not of this world.

You can be sure of My presence when you feel peace.

You can be sure that dreams come true as I open doors for you.

You can be sure of direction when I provide people or circumstances along your path when you pay attention.

My direction is steady and sure.

You can be sure that My love for you never changes.

My love for you is eternal.

You can be sure that I am with you. You only need to believe it.

Thanks

When you live your life with a grateful heart, you find goodness, strength, and peace.

Start your day by giving thanks.

Give thanks for a new beginning.

Give thanks for a roof over your head and food and water to drink.

Give thanks for family, friends, and loved ones.

End your day by giving thanks.

Give thanks for challenges and victories.

Give thanks for a place to rest.

I delight in your thanks and praise.

Time

Time is not in short supply.

Everyone has the same amount of time each day.

Use your time wisely.

Spend time with Me. I will renew your spirit.

Know that there is a time and purpose for everything.

There will be a time for gladness and a time for sorrow.

There is a time for planting, a time for tending, and a time for reaping.

Will you spend your time on mindless activities or being mindful in each moment?

Time and time again I will remind you of your significance and worthiness.

Make your time count.

Time is precious. *You* are precious.

Today

Today you have a new start. Yesterday is gone and tomorrow is yet to come.

What have you learned from the past that can help you today?

What do you want to accomplish today?

Today is a gift of twenty-four precious hours. Begin today with thoughts of gratitude.

Before you rush out, give thanks for what you have.

Today, make time for love and laughter.

Appreciate all that surrounds you.

When today is done, end today with more thoughts of gratitude. Ask yourself, "Did I live today, did I love today, did I give today, did I make today matter?"

Truly

Truly, if you believe what I say you will:

Truly find peace,

Truly experience joy,

Truly find purpose,

Truly know love.

When you trust in Me and allow Me to work on your behalf, you will truly experience a life of ease and freedom.

I know that it is truly hard for you to give up control.

You can only truly control so much.

Remember, I am in charge so that you can truly live life to the fullest.

Trust

Trust is the rock-solid foundation to a loving relationship.

Shattered trust is shattering faith and hope.

Shattered trust causes you to put on armor of self-protection and live on shaky, unstable ground.

You can put your trust in Me.

Investing small deposits of time in prayer, spending time in My presence, and thinking about My love for you throughout your day, translates to making small deposits of trust. Those deposits turn into a solid foundation of trust which can never be shattered.

When you learn to trust Me, I will help you discern with whom you should put your trust.

When you make good choices, you will trust yourself.

Trust yourself.

Trust others.

Trust Me.

Unique

Rejoice! You are unique!

You have unique gifts, talents, and strengths.

You have a unique way that you speak.

You have unique features.

You have unique preferences.

You and I have a unique relationship.

There is no one else like you!

When you compare yourself to others, you cause yourself pain.

So, be the most wonderful and unique you that you can be.

I treasure you!

The unique and amazing, one-of-a-kind *you*.

Unless

Unless you open your eyes to really see, you will miss beauty that is all around you.

You will miss signs that I provide to you.

Unless you open your ears, you will not hear life's music, words of love, and wisdom.

Unless you open your mind, you will miss the opportunity to expand and grow.

Unless you open your heart, you will miss out on what it feels like to be loved and to love in return.

Unless you stop your striving and slow your frantic pace, you will miss out on the peace and blessings I have in store for you.

Unlimited

I want to fill your life with:

Unlimited love,

Unlimited joy,

Unlimited abundance,

Unlimited possibilities,

Unlimited opportunities.

My patience for you is unlimited.

My love for you is unlimited.

My blessings for you are unlimited.

When you comprehend your spirit and My Spirit as
one, you will discover a life that is unlimited, unbridled, and free.

Valuable

What is valuable in *My* kingdom is different from what is considered valuable in the material world.

You may collect valuable possessions.

No matter what the expense, they can't compare to valuable, loving relationships.

They can't compare to the valuable time you spend with Me.

What is more valuable than love, peace, compassion, health, and well-being?

When you spend time with Me, I will give you valuable insights.

Look at the birds and how I take care of their every need.

Do you not know how much more valuable *you* are to Me?

Never forget how valuable you are, or the valuable and unique gifts and talents you possess.

Share these valuable gifts with the world.

Virtue

When you put your mind on things that are good, honest, just, lovely and pure, you develop virtue.

By virtue of having My power and goodness within you, you have power and goodness.

Cultivating virtue is an admirable quality.

When you live your life in the highest integrity, you will draw people and opportunities to you.

By virtue of your actions, people will not only come to know you, but they will come to know Me.

Virtue will support you and empower you.

Will

I have given you free will. That's because I love you with an unconditional love.

I know that you seek to do *My will,* but that causes confusion. A parent never forces their will on their children. That is not true love.

My will is supporting *your will* in the gifts and talents you've been given.

Nothing thrills Me more than seeing My children step into the people I created them to be.

That is *My will* for you.

I will always love you.

I will always support you.

I will always help you.

You, however, must choose to be willing.

Wish

I gave you free will so that you can do whatever you wish.

I wish for you to fully understand what that means.

What action you take is up to you.

Every action has a consequence that results in an outcome that is either beneficial or harmful for you.

What you wish is up to you.

By the way, I am not a genie who says, "Your wish is My command."

It doesn't work that way. You must do your part.

However, know that I:

Wish the best for you,

Wish happiness for you,

Wish fulfillment for you,

Wish peace for you.

Wish greatness for you.

Above all, I wish you could fathom how much I love and care for you.

I Am

I say that I Am, but you may not understand what I mean.

I Am your Strength.

I Am your Rock.

I Am your Shelter.

I Am your Peace.

I Am your Provider.

I Am your Protector.

I Am your Creator, so you can create like Me.

I Am Truth.

I Am Love.

I Am always with you; always loving you.

Acknowledgements

I can't possibly list all the people I wish to thank, or that would be another book! But I do wish to acknowledge several key people. Without their encouragement and contribution, this book would not be in front of your eyes: My husband, Robert Trottmann, who gave me the greatest gift to quit my job to write. Caroline Revelo published my first book and started my writing career. Rita, my first spiritual director, guided me on the path to healing and wholeness. Paul Reiter, my spiritual director, companion, and friend who walks along side of me. My pastors, David Holyan and Karen Blanchard for their inspiration, knowledge, love, and support. For First Presbyterian Church of Kirkwood, Missouri where I've made wonderful friends, am spiritually fed, nurtured, and honored to serve.

Jared Rosen saw my meditation work and God Notes as a remedy to the frenzied, fast-paced, stress-filled lifestyle that our culture promotes. Thank you, Jared, for sharing my vision, for mentoring me through the entire publishing process, and guiding me through the greatest challenge of all—what happens *after* the book is finished.

Thank you, Darlene Swanson, for your collaboration and bringing God Notes to life through your beautiful design.

Without Terry Anglin, there would be no following for my writing. Terry helped me set up my websites and blog. He rescued me through my perils with technology. I owe Terry a debt of gratitude. Terry is a friend, mentor, and true example of what it means to live out his Christian faith.

Thank you to all of my blog readers, The Guided Life Ezine readers, and Facebook followers. Your love and encouragement in return has been such a blessing to me. I especially wish to thank Judee, Patti, Carol, Nancy, JoAnne, Shelley, Loretta, Rachelle, Chris, Kathleen, Daniel, Bev, Joan, Steve, Sarah, Deloris, Kimberly, Bob and Mary, Jane, Mike, and Lynette, along with my support group of Jeff, Jill, Aprille, Tom, Gina, and Anthony. Thank you, George Kelly, for being God's angel sent whenever times got rough. You helped me to persevere.

I give thanks for my constant friend, Denise Klose. We've weathered our careers and lots of life's storms together along with sharing lots of love and laughter. Thank you for your love and support.

A huge thank you to my audio producer, Richard Del Maestro for your coaching and direction. You've been an angel sent by God too.

Thank you, Clarence Heller, for introducing me to the month-long prayer retreat and to my prayer companion Kristie. What a surprise and blessing that this work became the fruit from that time of stillness and prayer. And, finally, thank you God from whom all blessings, love, and inspiration flows.

About the Author

J ackie Trottmann left her corporate career behind to pursue God's call to share her personal experience of God's healing power and loving presence. Learning how to be still, let go, trust herself, trust others, and trust God, has been an ongoing spiritual practice. She teaches others how to do the same through her books, blog, meditation CDs, speaking, workshops, and other writing. Jackie's greatest joy is found with pen and notebook in hand expressing God's latest inspiration, or behind a microphone recording the next project. Jackie shares her life and love of travel with husband, Robert.

Connect with Jackie through JackieTrottmann.com

Visit GodNotes.net

Made in the USA
Lexington, KY
19 May 2017